W.B. YEATS

SEANAD EIREANN

SPEECHES

1922 - 1928

by

Michael Manning

To Eugene Paul Dunne (1924 – 2014)

Even were I to rise up to Heaven, Thou art there. Even were I to descend into hell, Thou art there. Yeah, even were I to make my abode in the depths of the sea, there too would Thy right hand reach me!

An extract from: The Russian Orthodox Church Cathechism.

Published by Lulu.com

Content ID: 10116859

Copyright Michael Manning

Published by Lulu.com

ISBN 978-1-4467-9512-5

The author correctly credits all photographs used in this book. References and sources are listed in the index at the back of the book.

Michael Manning holds a B.A.Mod., M.A. and H.Dip. Education from Trinity College Dublin and is currently a freelance Science and Technical Journalist and Translator encouraging science and scientific writing in all forms of modern media.

CONTENTS

W.B. Yeats Seanad Eireann Speeches, 1922-28 - 8

Seanad Eirean - 10

12th December, 1923. Election of Chairman - 14

10th January, 1923. Advisory Committees - 14

24th January, 1923. Indemnity (British Military) Bill - 15

8th February, 1923. Enforcement of Law Bill - 16

14th March, 1923. The Griffith Settlement Bill - 17

15th March, 1923. Local Government Bill - 17

22nd March, 1923. Electoral Bill - 18

28th March, 1923. Damage to Property Bill - 19

18th April, 1923. Compensation for Personal Injuries - 20

19th April, 1923. The League of Nations - 20

19th April, 1923. Irish Manuscripts – 20

9th May, 1923. The Lane Pictures -23

6th June, 1923. Oireachtas Payment of Members Bill – 26

7th June, 1923. Censorship of Films Bill – 26

25th June, 1923. National Health Insurance Bill – 26

11th July, 1923. Accommodation for Oireachtas – 27

26th July, 1923. Public Safety Emergency Powers Bill – 27

3rd August, 1923. Land Bill Report Stage - 27

14th November, 1923. Sir Horace Plunkett's Resignation – 27

14th November, 1923. Report of the Committee on Standing Orders – 28

15th January, 1924. Civil Service Regulation – 28

15th January, 1924. Irish Language – 29

15th January, 1924. Saorstat Representation, British Empire Exhibition-30

23rd January, 1924. Public Safety(Powers of Arrest and Detention)Bill-30

6th February, 1924. Courts of Justice Bill - 30

19th March, 1924. Ministers and Secretaries Bill, National Gallery – 30

19th March, 1924. Ministers and Secretaries Bill – 31

3rd April, 1924. Ministers and Secretaries Bill – 31

1st May, 1924. Report on Temporary Accommodation the Oireachtas –33

21st May, 1924. Future Business – 34

4th June, 1924. Peril to National Museum from Fire – 34

4th June, 1924. Final Report of Committee on Irish Manuscripts – 35

19th June, 1924. Temporary Accommodation of the Oireachtas - 43

2nd July, 1924. Railways Bill 1924, Third Stage – 44

3rd July, 1924. Finance Bill, 1924; Second Stage – 45

16th July, 1924. Temporary Accommodation of the Oireachtas – 46

16th July, 1924. National Museum & Adjoining Buildings FireDanger–49

17th October, 1924. Solution of Outstanding National Problems – 50

10th June, 1925. Shannon Electricity Bill 1925 Third Stage – 51

11th June, 1925. Debate on Divorce Legislation – 47

17th December, 1925. Civil Service Regulation Bill 1925 – 53

3rd March, 1926. Coinage Bill 1926 Second Stage - 54

24th March, 1926. School Attendance Bill Second Stage 1926 – 54

30th March, 1926. Central Fund Bill, Second Stage, 1926 – 59

26th April, 1926. School Attendance Bill, 1925, Third Stage – 61

15th June, 1926. Message from the Dail. – 62

14th July, 1926. The Lane Pictures – 64

22nd July, 1926. High Court and Supreme Court Rules – 69

24th February, 1927. Industrial and Commercial Property Bill 1926 – 73

9th March, 1927. Merrion Square, (Dublin) Bill, 1927 – 73

11th March, 1927. Industrial and Commercial Property Bill, 1926, 3rd Stage – 75

7th April, 1927. Merrion Square (Dublin) Bill 1927 – 81

4th May, 1927. Industrial and Commercial Property (Protection) Bill 1926 Report Stage – 82

4th May, 1927. Industrial and Commercial Property (Protection) Bill (Resumed) – 82

18th July, 1928. Constitution (Amendment No. 6) Bill, 1928, Fifth Stage – 88

Conclusion-88

Photographs - Autograph Tree – 89, Thoor Ballylee, Gort, Co Galway – 90

Seanad Members Database 1922 – 1925; - 91

Seanad Members Database 1925 – 1928; - 96

Sources and References - 101

Sources Seanad Eireann Debates and Speeches – 101

W.B. Yeats Seanad Eireann Speeches, 1922-28

William Butler Yeats (1865-1939) is regarded as the most quoted poet in the English language of the twentieth and twenty first century. Yeats produced more memorable lines and phrases than any other modern writer. Most Irish schoolchildren were introduced to Yeats poetry by means of the Leaving Certificate book *Soundings,* edited by Augustine Martin. Fortunately, this book returns to the Irish School curriculum in 2011. Automatic learning and reciting poetry was not encouraged by Yeats, however, the lure of his enduring poetry remains.

Many of Yeats phrases entered newspaper headlines, articles and word of mouth. Nature documentary film maker Gerrit van Gelderen used Yeats 'To the Waters and the Wild' as the title for a wildlife documentary series of films from The Stolen Child poem, thereby popularising his legacy. 'A terrible beauty'; 'fumble in a greasy till'; 'Romantic Ireland is dead and Gone, it is with O'Leary in the Grave' are memorable. Yeats ensured his primary purpose of the poet was to create memorable speech 'to articulate sweet sounds together.'

Yeats founded and joined societies all his life, striving to develop a group of Irish writers in order to escape from being subsumed as English Literature. The major collaboration with fellow writer Lady Augusta Gregory was the founding of the Abbey Theatre in 1904. The idea came to them in Count de Basterot's, Doorus House, Kinvara, Co Galway in the summer of 1897. The designation Ireland's National Theatre was controversial. Yeats wanted artists, poets and writers to express the oral Irish tradition on the national stage.

Yeats and Lady Gregory projected a utopian future when they co-wrote and produced the play, Cathleen ni Houlihan in 1902 with the electrifying personification of Ireland by Maud Gonne on stage. The leaders of the Easter 1916 rebellion were writers, poets, playwrights and visionaries with Cu Chulainn as an icon central to the reawakening of a suppressed national consciousness. Yeats was annoyed he was not consulted about the rebellion.

W. B. Yeats was born in Sandymount, Dublin in 1865, his early life was dominated by his father, John Butler Yeats, abandoning a lucrative career in law for the careworn life as a portrait painter. The Yeats family moved between Dublin and London as much as James Joyce moved around Dublin, leading a vicarious life. Yeats shared Joyce's laconic description of Ireland 'Great hatred, little room' comparing with James Joyce's 'The

Peat Rick, where Church and Caesar rule hand in glove.' Stability was guaranteed with summer stays at the Polloxfen grand parent's home in Sligo. The natural beauty and stories from the local people stimulated the young Yeats. Art and the artist were cultivated. Ireland's greatest poet W.B. Yeats and most accomplished artist Jack B. Yeats came from this background.

Yeats love for Maud Gonne, who rejected his marriage proposals twice, inspired his greatest love poetry. Yeats latterly married George Hyde-Lees who shared his interest in the occult remaining the only other language he knew. Yeats inspired John Millington Synge to write about Aran, a place no one had written about previously, inspiring his six plays of Aran Island life, including The Playboy of the Western World (1907).

Yeats spent three years in England after 1916 and purchased a Norman tower, Thoor Ballylee near Coole Park, Gort Co Galway. The 1922-24 Civil War raged yet Yeats remained at Thoor Ballylee.

Yeats was advised to live in a warmer climate during the winter months, so, he did not serve a third term in the Senate. In later life Yeats became quite controversial rejecting Sean O'Casey's The Silver Tassie. Yeats initially supported the Blueshirts but soon found O'Duffy a ludicrous figure. Yeats died in Rocquebrune France, January 1939 and was reinterred in Drumcliffe Churchyard, County Sligo after the war as per his will.

Seanad Eireann

Seanad Eireann, the Irish Senate, was set up in December 1922 to provide some stability in the country. Sinn Fein (Ourselves Alone), the political party, was split by the pro-Treaty and anti-Treaty factions. A government was set up 14th January 1922. In August 1922 Griffith died and Collins was shot at an ambush. The only able leader left standing was W.T. Cosgrave who led the non party government until, on 7th December 1922 exactly one year and one day after the Treaty was signed, a meeting to form the new party in Parnell Square, Dublin, was attacked by 6 gunmen, General Sean Hales died. On 27th April 1923 Cumann na nGaedheal was established and remained in government 1923 – 33.

W.T. Cosgrave, an able administrator, achieved a lot and managed to stabilise a divided country. An Garda Siochana, an unarmed police force, was created before the Civil War was finalised. The tremendous Shannon electrification scheme was launched at great cost. The Cumann na nGaedhael party defended Irish constitutional nationalism from Republican and Free State dissension. Ireland joined the League of Nations to enhance the Free State's reputation abroad. The 1926 Imperial Conference ensured Irish sovereignty was enhanced. These remarkable achievements were secured following a bloodily divisive Civil War.

The intellectual aristocratic make up of the Senate was in stark contrast to the nationalistic, farming background of the ever strident establishment of a Catholic Irish Free State. Yeats challenged the Ireland of his times during a fractious Irish Civil War when a number of landowning Protestant Senators had their property burned to the ground. Foreign Minister O'Higgins was shot dead in 1927. Yeats composed his Senate speeches in Thoor Ballylee near Gort, Co Galway.

The worst of times led to the opportunity for Yeats when the Free State government established a Senate in an attempt to stabilise the country. Yeats accepted the appointment as Senator and served two successive terms of three years each from 1922 to 1928. Yeats gave his first Senate speech on 12th December 1922 in support of the proposal of Lord Glenavy as Cathaoirleach (Chairman) of the House. Glenavy, an outstanding lawyer, and a Unionist, opposed Home Rule and was at variance with the overwhelming Nationalist sentiment of the country. Yeats proposed they were members of the Senate and neither Unionist and Nationalist. In 1923 Yeats spoke nineteen times on law enforcement, Irish manuscripts, the Lane paintings, film censorship and the Irish language, his allies were Protestant Unionists supported by his father's friend, Andrew Jameson of Jameson Distillery. In a speech on law enforcement, 8th February 1923 Yeats warned against the extension of officers rights to enter private houses and adds an account of his own personal experiences in Co Galway.

'He had with him seven Free State soldiers to protect him…. Shortly afterwards, however, he found himself amongst debtors who were less hospitable, they compelled him to eat all his own summonses, There was a large quantity of paper, and paper, I believe, is extremely indigestible.'

In March 1923 a bill came before the Senate to make provision for the family of Arthur Griffith. Of course Griffith antagonised Yeats over The Playboy of the Western World, yet Yeats paid him an eloquent tribute: 'He gave his faith, not to an abstract theory, but to the conception of this historical nation – we are all theory mad.'

Yeas regarded his first year in the Senate as the most rewarding of his life, he was awarded an honorary D.Litt. by Dublin University in December 1922. Yeats contributed to a range of topics. In particular, the fate of the French Impressionist paintings acquired by Lady Gregory's Hugh Lane and intended for display in a special purpose built gallery. Lane bequeathed the collection to the National Gallery in London but Lane was persuaded to change his mind, entering an un-witnessed codicil reversing his decision in Dublin's favour. Lane died on the Lusitania in 1915. Yeats raised this subject frequently in the Senate. Twenty years after his death, in 1959, a joint agreement was reached whereby the Lane paintings were rotated every six months between Dublin and London.

Yeats spoke on government censorship, on literature and film and was appointed committee chairman designing Irish coins. The familiar animals on Irish coinage duly followed.

President W.T. Cosgrave of Cumann na nGaedheal, sought to bring in a law requiring women to retire from the public service on marriage. Yeats spoke out on discouraging marriage due to discrimination against women in the Senate. Yeats was interested in the education of children with the child the object of education. Yeats spoke on the decision to outlaw divorce in a provocative and entertaining manner which was mischievously delivered. Yeats was determined to challenge the increasingly Catholic Free State and remind them of his Protestant origins.

In 1925, Yeats made a strident speech on the subject of Northern Ireland and its partition from the Free State, urging the Free State to meet the northern counties in counsel. 'I have no hope of seeing Ireland united in my time, or of seeing Ulster won in my time; but I believe it will be won in the end, and not because we fight it, but because we govern this country well.'

Yeats advocated the theories of Mussolini's new Italian State's education minister Gentile, in the Irish Senate along with the doctrines of Croce. In May 1925 Yeats prepared his celebrated speech on divorce in Thoor Ballylee which he delivered on 11th June to a disconcerted Senate. Perhaps Yeats had a wry sense of humour, being perchance arrogantly divisive? Yeats was certainly prophetic, apolitical, yet he sought to address the long term future of Ireland: 'We against whom you have done this thing are no petty people. We are one of the great stocks of Europe. We are the people of Burke; we are the people of Grattan; we are the people of Swift, the people of Emmet and the people of Parnell…. If we have not lost our stamina then your victory will be brief, and your defeat final, and when it comes, this country will be transformed.'

Yeats wrote a letter describing his beliefs in the late 1930s: 'Do not make a politician of me, even in Ireland I shall never I think be that again – as my sense of reality deepens, and I think it does with age, my horror at the cruelty of governments grows greater. Communist, fascist, nationalist, clerical, anti-clerical, are all responsible according to the number of their victims.'

Yeats was advised to live in a warmer climate during the winter months, so, he did not serve a third term in the Senate. Yeats attended the second Seanad Eireann term less regularly due to increasing ill health. He defended Joyce's Ulysses from copyright violations and spoke on Merrion Square, Copyright and other topics until 18th July, 1928.

Fianna Fail's de Valera abolished the Senate in 1936, his 1937 Constitution provided for a new upper house, the Seanad. In 2011 the less than eloquent Seanad Eireann is threatened with closure. The Seanad became a repository for those who lost their seats in Dail Eireann. An Taoiseach de Valera set a precedent, suspending Seanad Eireann for three years. Seanad Eireann is less than democratic with An Taoiseach nominating 11 members and two University panels selecting three each.

Most people in debt plagued Ireland of 2011 disregard politics and politicians offhand. Politicians do not make any attempt to be relevant. A generous salary and severance pay a long with unverifiable expenses discredit many who climb the greasy pole of power and politics. Ireland will survive its difficulties hopefully with its optimistic people unbowed.

12th December, 1923. Election of Chairman

Mr. YEATS: 'I think we should put aside once and for all diplomacy in dealing with the people of the country. We have been diplomatised for a generation. Let us stop it. I am in thorough agreement with Colonel Moore when he said we would be judged in this country by our abilities as a Seanad. I suggest we consider nothing whatever but whether the man we are going to choose will have the necessary legal and necessary political knowledge to steer this Seanad through the exceedingly intricate channels through which it will have to pass. We have thorny legal questions in this Seanad on every side of us, and, of course, we will have thorny political questions. The past is dead not only for us but for this country. There is no individual we can appoint who will add in any way to our popularity. What enemy of ours will lay down his gun because of any man we appoint here? I suggest we are assembled here no longer in a Nationalist or Unionist sense, but merely as members of the Seanad.'

10th January, 1923 Advisory Committees

Mr. YEATS: 'I have felt, and I am sure we have all felt, the fact that we are a group of individuals who do not know each other, and that is a great injury to us in our capacity as a deliberative body. I think, at the same time, if Colonel Moore brings this to a vote now it will probably be lost, and I imagine under the new Standing Orders it would not be possible to raise it again for some time. I think it is necessary for us to know something of each other before we form such a Committee on the various subjects suggested by Colonel Moore. I feel it is important that we should not do anything now to injure our chances of carrying out such a project later on. I think, then, we might possibly find it a little desirable to be guided by the idea of not forming Committees on subjects for which there are already Ministers in the Dáil. Now, if we appoint Committees such as those suggested, we may find ourselves in the position of critics of the Dáil, which is not desirable. We might, on the other hand, find it desirable to form Committees for subjects in connection with which there are no Ministries. For instance, Public Health. Now there is no Ministry of Public Health. It might be desirable to form Committees of that kind. I am myself anxious to see a Committee appointed to look after the interests of Fine Arts, and I do feel if this motion is brought to a vote it may probably be lost, and if it is not lost we have not sufficient knowledge of each other to form such Committees with the necessary information. I therefore suggest that we postpone this resolution for some time.' Yeats was appointed to the Standing Committee.

24th January, 1923. Indemnity (British Military) Bill

Mr. YEATS: 'I think we must simply act on the information we have, and try and come to a decision that seems to us right on the arguments before us. If we do cause inconvenience to the Dáil, the Dáil will possibly find some means of putting the facts as they see them before us. We can only act on the facts as they are before us now. I would suggest that we are not making anything in the nature of a threat. We are simply suggesting to England that this amnesty should be made in the most gracious form possible, and that it could only be made in the most gracious form by being made by both countries. I presume that both England and we have the same object to allay the bitter feeling between these countries, and we have drawn the attention of the English Parliament to an unfortunate oversight on their part. They have omitted to set free certain prisoners whom they have, perhaps, forgotten. We think that this amnesty upon our part will sound better in the ears of our won countrymen if England passes a similar amnesty. I think that is a very fair conclusion to come to. I think it is also very important to this Seanad, because of the very nature of its constitution, that we should show ourselves as interested as the Dáil is in every person in this country. We do not represent constituencies; we are drawn together to represent certain forms of special knowledge, certain special interests, but we are just as much passionately concerned in these great questions as the Dáil. I would suggest, therefore, that we pass this resolution now.'

8th February, 1923. Enforcement of Law Bill

Mr. YEATS: "'I would draw attention to the following:—'Provided however that in any case where the Under-Sheriff shall break and enter the premises of a person other than the person against whom he has been called upon to enforce a judgment order or decree he shall either have found any goods, animals or other chattels of such last-mentioned person therein or thereon or shall have reasonable grounds for believing that there were some such goods, animals or chattels therein or thereon.'

As I understood from the speech of the Minister, this is the clause that has been strengthened. In its original form he was only exempt from action if he did find goods in the house, such as he expected to find. At present he can evade on showing reasonable grounds of suspicion. I raise the point that it is a very serious thing to increase the rights of entry into a house. You have here the case where an officer of the State can enter a house. You increase the rights of entry, and that is a serious thing. I do not say that it is wrong to do. At present it seems to me that the bailiff can enter your house and allege that his reason for doing so is that he suspects you of having a clock belonging to a neighbour against whom there is a judgment. I think it is a serious thing to give the bailiff the right to enter your house, possibly by force, because of the suspicion he holds that you have got somebody else's property. Unless there is some very strong reason for it, I would ask the Minister to consider a modification of the clause.

The general necessity of this Bill leaves in my mind no possibility of doubt. About 6 months ago I was staying in the country, when a process server arrived to serve a process on me. I think it was for rates. He had with him seven Free State soldiers to protect him. I invited him to tea, and he and the Free State soldiers had tea with me, and my wife took their photographs. Shortly afterwards, however, he found himself amongst debtors who were less hospitable, for instead of giving him tea and cake and taking his photograph, they compelled him to eat all his own summonses. There was a large quantity of paper, and paper, I believe, is exceedingly indigestible. On the question of the details of the Bill I have nothing to say, as the representative of the Labour Party has drawn attention to the one clause which rouses my suspicion only because I do not yet know whether there is a very good case for it.'
'I think the principle is that the Minister for Justice Kevin O'Higgins, can be changed if he does an unpopular act. He can go away, taking the bitterness he has raised with him, but the Civic Guard cannot be changed.'

14th March, 1923. The Griffith Settlement Bill

Mr. YEATS: 'I wish to add my voice to that of Senator Colonel Sir Hutcheson Poe. I was on many points deeply opposed to Mr. Arthur Griffith during his lifetime on matters connected with the Arts, but time has justified him on the great issue that most concerns us all. He was a man with the most enduring courage and the most steadfast will. I have good reason for knowing how enduring his courage was. I first met him a great many years ago, when he and his friend Rooney were editing a little paper which they set up with their own hand as well as writing it. They also paid for the weekly expenditure on that paper. I know how hard a struggle it was for him to edit and print that paper, and I remember in those days, on hearing how hard that struggle was, I offered to get some of his articles placed in, I think, "The Speaker," which was an English Liberal paper. I remember his reply, that he had taken a vow to himself never to write for any paper outside Ireland. That was for him a vow of poverty, and he kept it. For many years, at least two or three years, before the end, it must have seemed to him that he was carrying on an almost hopeless struggle and when the final crisis came he showed himself a man of particular value to this country, if it were only in this, that when the final test came he gave his faith, not to an abstract theory, but to a conception of this historical nation — and we are all theory mad. On that point he kept himself thoroughly sane, and we owe, therefore, to his memory great honour— honour that will always be paid by this country.'

15th March, 1923. Local Government Bill

Mr. YEATS: 'In moving my amendment I am not going to use the form of words which has been circulated. These words are not mine, and I do not think them practicable, so I hope I have the leave of the Seanad to use a different form of words which in no way differs in intention from that circulated. I propose that in addition to the message to the Dáil proposed in paragraph 5 a message be also forwarded requesting that before any final arrangements are made relative to the permanent location of the Oireachtas, including the questions of site, locality, and the allocation of the necessary chambers and offices between the two Houses, a joint conference of members of both Houses be called together to consider this matter. I know, of course, that as this is a matter that involves the expenditure of money, the other House will be entirely within its rights if it refuses to consult us on the matter, but I would think now that it is pointed to them they will decide as a matter of courtesy to consult us, for, after all, it is right that we should know in what manner of house we are going to speak and eat, and, if the state of this country continues to be disturbed, possibly to sleep. I, for one, would very much like to know, whether we are to have chairs or benches. I feel strongly in the circumstances in favour of benches. We only know from common rumour, if that can be described as knowledge, where the other House is to be. There is a certain amount of feeling in the country that it should be the House in College Green, and I am sure that, considering the strength of the case in sentiment and tradition for that House, if the Government has given up that idea they have done so for some sound reason. Then, we hear again from public rumour that we are probably going to the Royal Hospital. If that is decided upon I should like to be assured that the Government will take great care of that priceless building, that they will not alter it in any substantial way, and that if they have to add to it, as they will have, they will not so add to it as to destroy its proportions. It is a masterpiece of architecture. It is not only the work of a great architect, but the work of a great architect of a great period. There are also, I know, certain plaster ceilings there, Italian work of great value. But whatever decision they come to they should, as a matter of courtesy, consult us. It would be a matter to us of regret if it is found that the old building in College Green is impossible. I think that there are certain members of the Seanad present whose ancestors took part in the debates in that House, and helped to create one of the few great schools of oratory which has arisen since classical times. I think that if it were upon that ground alone the Government should consult us before it has made any final decision.'

22nd March, 1923. Electoral Bill

Mr. YEATS: 'I merely wish to point out that the proposal contains no suggestion that the photograph need be a recent one. The enterprising elector could put a photograph of himself as a baby on a card and, as all babies look exactly alike to the masculine mind, it will be impossible to say whether it was accurate or not.'

28th March, 1923. Damage to Property Bill

Mr. YEATS: 'If it comes to a vote on the question of compensation for personal injuries I do not know on which side I am going to vote, because as yet I have heard no defence of the Government position. I have failed to find any defence of the Government's position in the newspapers. I am convinced that they have a defence, because I have found through my life a certain dogma very valuable, "There is no strong case without a strong answer," and the whole country is full of cases for compensation for personal injuries. It is full even of excellent jokes on the subject. I am told that a certain country solicitor, acting for the widow of a murdered man, has sent into the Government a bill for a very badly perforated suit of clothes. Now, I think that the Government which receives with equanimity a claim of that kind has obviously a very strong case indeed, and I hope that the Minister for Finance will give us that case. I am very anxious to be instructed on what side I am to vote. Am I to assist the Seanad to hold up this Bill or not on this most important question? I do not know if I am in agreement with the Senator who is anxious that where a man's house has been burned he should be given the opportunity, instead of rebuilding, of building house property in some neighbouring town. I suggest that that would be an incitement to other men to burn their neighbours' houses and get rid of men who are occupying a certain amount of land that they would like. I also suggest that it is very desirable that any clause in this Bill which encourages a man to rebuild should be kept. This country will not always be an uncomfortable place for a country gentleman to live in, and it is most important that we should keep in this country a certain leisured class. I am afraid that Labour disagrees with me in that. On this matter I am a crusted Tory. I am of the opinion of the ancient Jewish book which says "there is no wisdom without leisure."'

18th April, 1923. Compensation for Personal Injuries

Mr. YEATS: 'In commenting on what the last Senator said, I wish to say that a letter appeared in the London *Times* about three weeks ago from some person acting for refugees, saying the Government was excluding compensation for personal injuries in order that loyalists injured in the late war might be left penniless. I think that is an example of the kind of misunderstanding the Government has to face over this Bill. I do not think anyone of us doubts for one moment that the tribunal the Government will set up will be perfectly just in this matter. It is a question of dealing with a country which is exceedingly suspicious, and refugees who are exceedingly suspicious, and the circumstances are such as likely to leave these suspicions in existence for a considerable time.'

19th April, 1923. The League of Nations

Mr. YEATS: 'I hold the same view as Senator Jameson, and I have risen to ask if it would not be expedient for the Seanad to appoint a Committee to go into the whole question especially with a view to considering the question of the Boundary, and as to what extent our entering the League of Nations would commit us to join in a war against our will. There are other most thorny subjects which to me seem to be questions for legal interpretation. I think it highly desirable that we should appoint a Committee with the necessary expert knowledge to report on the subject before we come to a definite decision.'

A fractious exchange ended with Mr. Yeats withdrawing the suggestion.

19th April, 1923. Irish Manuscripts

Mr. YEATS: 'In the old days in Ireland when we began our imaginative movement which, for good or evil, had a little share in bringing about recent events, we all looked forward to the time when there would be adequate editions of the old literature of Ireland. That literature is of very great importance. The late d'Arbois de Jubainville, a very great Frenchman of science, whom I knew, spent his life in its study on the ground that through that literature you got to know what the world was immediately before Homer. In addition to that there is lyric poetry, great lyric poetry in Irish, lyric literature that was matured in the time of Chaucer. The work I hope the Seanad will enable the various scholars to do will be a work of science, that is to say a study of a language which is of great importance to culture, and a study of this old literature. It is not a work of propaganda. I am not in any way denying the importance of propaganda, but personally I do not get any pleasure when I see my name spelt in a way that makes it look very strange to me at the top of this resolution. It seems to me that that is a course entirely warranted by recent science. It is the propagandist way of saying "I am getting better and better." What I propose to you is a work which I think any Government in the world would feel justified in undertaking. Much of this work has already been done by certain bodies, done with very limited resources, by the Royal Irish Academy, Trinity College, the School of Irish Learning and the Irish Texts Society. The greater portion of the Saga literature has already been adequately translated and adequately edited, but there still remains great quantities of old Bardic poetry which should be translated. There is also great need for critical additions of the Annals, the Annals of Boyle, Innisfallen and Connaught, and above all, perhaps there is need for a dictionary of the old language. I have been in consultation during the last week with the principal Gaelic scholars, or most of them. Mr. Best, Professor MacNeill, Dr. Douglas Hyde, and Mr. Gwynn. I think they are unanimous on the importance of the dictionary. Then, too, as a preliminary work, a proper catalogue is required of the work of the Royal Irish Academy. A very large rough catalogue does exist, but a condensed catalogue is necessary. Trinity College scholars have just published their catalogue, and the British Museum is about to publish its catalogue of Irish Manuscripts there.

The proposal I make will not require a very large sum of money. At the beginning, at any rate, it will be quite a small sum annually, which will be used to keep at their work certain young scholars. I understand that Professor Bergin of the National University has two or three scholars of very great promise. At the moment two of these are studying in Germany with travelling scholarships, I understand Professor O'Rahilly and Professor Gwynn, in Trinity College, have a few more. In ordinary circumstances these scholars would have to accept, let us say, School Inspectorships, or something of that kind, and would be lost to Irish Scholarship. It is most desirable that a little money should be found in order that they should be set to do the work I have described, probably cataloguing in the first place, and dictionary making, and later on, or simultaneously, editing all the old Bardic poetry and bringing out critical editions of the Annals. When I read this resolution, you will find that I have made slight additions to it at the suggestion of certain scholars, chiefly Mr. Best. I may be a little out of order in doing that, but I hope you will permit it. I have added a clause which would permit a certain portion of the money being expended in training scholars in phonetics, so that they would be able to take down what of Irish literature still remains in the living tongue. It is quite possible that that is the most important work of all, because that old literature in songs and stories is dying out. It only exists, I understand, in its perfection where the people still think in Irish. As they become thoroughly bilingual even, it dies away, so that it is work that can be done to-day, and done next year and the year after, but very soon it will be a work which cannot be done at all. That is why, perhaps, it is most pressing.

I feel it strange that I, who am a non-Gaelic scholar, should be left to bring this proposal before the Seanad. I may say, to give a little weight to my words, that the greater portion of my own writings have been founded upon the old literature of Ireland. I have had to read it in translations, but it has been the chief illumination of my imagination all my life. The movement I am connected with, the whole poetic movement of modern Ireland, has drawn a great portion of its inspiration from the old Bardic literature. I think it is of great importance to set before our own people a task which they will feel naturally inclined to undertake. It is a great thing, when you find people wanting to learn anything, that you should encourage them to learn that, and not something else that they do not want to learn.

It is a moment, too, when we will have to build up again the idealism of Ireland. We have had the old form of wild, wasteful historic idealism. The country got into that position, but, like a spendthrift coming into possession of his inheritance, it has wasted that idealism in a year of civil war. We have to build up again in its place an idealism of labour and of thought and it is not asking much that the few hundreds a year necessary should be spent to begin what may grow to be a very important work of national scholarship, a work for which all the scholars of the world will be grateful, a work which will enhance the reputation of this country. I, therefore, propose the amendment in its amended form: "That a Committee of the Seanad be appointed to submit to the Government a scheme for the editing, indexing, and publishing of manuscripts in the Irish language now lying in the Royal Irish Academy, Trinity College and elsewhere; for the scientific investigation of the living dialects; for the compiling and publishing of an adequate dictionary of the older language; that the Committee have power to invite the assistance of persons not members of the Seanad, and to take evidence on the subject, the Committee to consist of four members of the Seanad." I am now able to add the names of four members, Senator MacLysaght, Senator Mrs. Green, Senator Mrs. Costello, and myself. I find it a little difficult to suggest a quorum because those members will add to their numbers persons——'

Yeats was made chairman of the committee.

9th May, 1923. The Lane Pictures

Mr. YEATS: 'I have the following motion to move:

"That the Seanad ask the Government to press upon the British Government the return to Dublin of the pictures mentioned in the unwitnessed codicil to Sir Hugh Lane's will."

This is an old question. We have been agitating now for some years, and I have some reason for saying that the opposition against the return of these pictures is dying away. I think the justice of our case has been generally admitted. It is simply a question of the inertia of Government and of giving them the necessary impulse towards arriving at some definite decision. It is necessary, however, I think, to remind you of the circumstances under which that codicil was written. A good many years ago now Sir Hugh Lane established in Dublin a famous gallery of modern pictures. When he established it there was no modern gallery here in which students could study, and they had to go abroad to do so. Sir Hugh Lane was no mere picture dealer, but in the words of an eminent authority, he lifted the trade of the picture dealer into the realm of art. He sold pictures merely that he might buy other pictures, and he bought pictures in order that he might endow a great gallery. After he made the Dublin Municipal Gallery the most important collection of French pictures outside Luxembourg, he was somewhat discourteously treated by some of the Dublin newspapers and certain persons, and an acrimonious controversy arose.

In 1913, under the impulse of that controversy, he made a will leaving certain pictures, generally known as the Hugh Lane French pictures, to the National Gallery of London. These pictures had been given to the Municipal Gallery conditional on certain requests being carried out. Those requests were not carried out, and he gave them to the English National Gallery. He felt the pictures were not valued here. He lent them to the English National Gallery to show that they were real pictures of worth. Then under irritation he made this will, by which he left all his property, with the exception of those French pictures, to the National Gallery of Ireland. He left certain pictures to the Municipal Gallery, but he left the French pictures to the London National Gallery. Two years later, in 1915, when he was going on a journey to America, which he knew to be dangerous, he made a codicil by which the National Gallery was to return the pictures known as French pictures back to Ireland. He wrote that codicil in ink. He signed it on each page. I have a photographic copy of it in my hand; when he made a slight correction in the date he initialled that correction. No document could be more formal except for one omission. He never had it witnessed. He spoke of this change of mind to various people. I have in this pamphlet three affidavits of how he spoke of changing his mind, and wishing that Ireland had his French pictures. Of his intention there can be no question whatever. From those various documents I think I may read you one affidavit made by his sister:

I, RUTH SHINE, of Lindsey House, 100 Cheyne Walk, London, S.W., widow, do solemnly and sincerely declare as follows:

The late Sir Hugh Lane was a brother of mine, and he is hereinafter referred to as "my brother."

In January, 1915, my brother spoke to me of making another will. He went to Dublin, however, without having done so. It was there (on February 3rd) that he wrote and signed his codicil and locked it in his desk at the National Gallery in a sealed envelope addressed to me; it was very clearly and carefully written and I have no doubt whatever that he considered it legal.

My brother had no ordinary business habits in the ordinary sense of the word, and was ignorant of legal technicalities. He dictated both his wills to me, the first leaving all to the Modern Art Gallery in Dublin, and the second leaving all to the National Gallery of Dublin, with the exception of the French pictures left to London. But for my persistence, neither would have been witnessed; even when he dictated the second will he had forgotten all I had told him about that necessity. So little am I surprised at there being no witnesses to the codicil that my surprise is altogether that he should have written it so carefully. He must have made rough drafts, as he composed letters with great difficulty, and the codicil was so well written.

I think from my knowledge of him that if he thought of a witness at all he would perhaps have considered that a codicil to an already witnessed will needed no further formality. When he sealed up the envelope he was going on a dangerous journey to America, and was so much impressed by that danger that at first he had refused to go at all unless those who had invited him for business reasons would insure his life for £50,000 to clear his estate of certain liabilities, and he thought he was going not in seven or eight weeks, as it happened, but in two or three.

I have approached this subject without any bias in favour of Dublin, but as his sister, anxious that his intentions should be carried out, and I make this declaration conscientiously believing the same to be true and by virtue of the provisions of the Statutory Declaration Act, 1835.

RUTH SHINE.

Declared at Markham House, King's Road, Chelsea, in the County of London, this 13th day of February, 1917.

Before me,

G.F. WILKINS,

A Commissioner for Oaths.

That codicil would have been legal in Scotland. It seems to us that a request made to a great Gallery is something different from a request made to an individual; that a great Gallery like this cannot desire to retain property which was left to it by accident, and that it must desire, as we do, the return of these pictures if they are set free by Act of Parliament legalising the codicil. We believe that that Act of Parliament can be obtained. One Irish Chief Secretary had prepared such a Bill, but it has been pushed aside by the pressure of Parliamentary business. It is very important for Ireland to recover these pictures. With the addition of the French pictures the Municipal Gallery is more than doubled in its importance, for those pictures are complementary to the pictures here in Dublin. He was not only a connoisseur; he had the gift of arranging pictures so as to display them to the best advantage. With those pictures there, we should have in the Municipal Gallery a possession which in future generations would draw people to Dublin, and help in enriching the city and the whole population by bringing those pilgrims. The actual money value of the pictures is hard to decide, because pictures constantly change their value, but about twelve years ago they were valued at about £75,000. It is quite probable they are worth more now. One picture, by Malet, Manet (Sic.), might be bought at £20,000 They also have this further importance: they will never be in the market again. The great pictures of that period in French art are already finding their way into national collections. It is precisely for that reason that certain English critics have tried to keep the pictures in England. They know that if they cannot keep these French pictures in London they can never have a representative collection of French art. In fighting to recover these pictures you are fighting for a unique possession which will always remain unique and always give prestige to the Gallery that contains it.'

6th June, 1923. Oireachtas Payment of Members Bill

Mr. YEATS: 'He said that the average of attendance had been 60 per cent. and that is very high. Many Senators have attended at great loss to themselves, and some with danger to themselves. This Seanad has a brief but honourable career. If you are to create and preserve a habit of service you must trust that habit and you must be ready to prefer integrity to any kind of weight and measure.'

During the first three months of 1923 some Senators' great houses were burned.

7th June, 1923 Censorship of Films Bill

Mr. YEATS: 'A terrible responsibility has been thrust upon me. I merely rose to say that I thought I could comfort the mind of the Senator who proposed this amendment. Artists and writers for a very long time have been troubled at intervals by their work. I remember John Synge and myself both being considerably troubled when a man, who had drowned himself in the Liffey, was taken from the river. He had in his pocket a copy of Synge's play, "Riders to the Sea," which, you may remember, dealt with a drowned man. We know, of course, that Goethe was greatly troubled when a man was taken from the river, having drowned himself. The man had in his pocket a copy of "Werther," which is also about a man who had drowned himself. It has again and again cropped up in the world that the arts do appeal to our imitative faculties. We comfort ourselves in the way Goethe comforted himself, that there must have been other men saved from suicide by having read "Werther." We see only the evil effect, greatly exaggerated in the papers, of these rather inferior forms of art which we are now discussing, but we have no means of reducing to statistics their other effects. I think you can leave the arts, superior or inferior, to the general conscience of mankind.'

Amendment put and negatived.

25th June, 1923. National Health Insurance Bill

Insufficient information was available to debate this motion.

11th July, 1923. Accommodation for Oireachtas

Mr. YEATS: 'I propose that that Committee be formed. I think that it should be clearly understood that in appointing this Committee, or in agreeing to sit upon it, we do not in any way commit ourselves to any decision about the site. I understand that plans are being prepared for Kilmainham, but I think it must be understood that we are quite free to object to that site, even as a temporary site. I do not say that I would recommend that, but we must go into it quite freely. I think most of us have a feeling that it is undesirable that Kilmainham should be the permanent site of an Irish Parliament. People coming up from the country, we feel, will want to find themselves nearer the Parliament than they would be if you put it out into a remote suburb.' Expert opinion was sought.

26th July, 1923 Public Safety Emergency Powers Bill

No objection to the inspection of prisons.

3rd August, 1923 Land Bill Report Stage

Inclusive of any monument of archaeological interest.

14th November, 1923 Sir Horace Plunkett's Resignation

Mr. YEATS: 'If I am in order, I wish to say how much the whole Seanad regrets Sir Horace Plunkett's resignation. I understand that the establishment of every technical school and agricultural college in this country is the result of his efforts, and we know that the methods of organisation which he perfected in Ireland have spread to a good many countries. In Ireland he organised, I think, 180,000 farmers into his organisation. If I remember rightly the last public letter of President Roosevelt, when he was President of the United States, was a letter of thanks to Sir Horace Plunkett for his great services to the organisation of agriculture in the United States. We, here, forget sometimes how great his work has been and how much honourable fame it has brought to this country.'

14th November, 1923. Report of the Committee on Standing Orders

Mr. YEATS: 'I wish to make a very emphatic protest against the histrionics which have crept into the whole Gaelic movement. People pretend to know a thing that they do not know and which they have not the smallest intention of ever learning. It seems to me to be discreditable and undesirable. I hope this will not be taken as being unsympathetic to the Gaelic movement. In the Abbey Theatre, on Monday night, a play in Irish was produced, and the theatre was packed with an enthusiastic audience. They knew Irish, and they were able to understand the language of the play, but I think this method of histrionics, and going through a childish performance of something we do not know, and which we do not intend to learn, will ultimately lead to a reaction against the language. I wish to say that I wish to see the country Irish speaking.'

15th January, 1924. Civil Service Regulation

Mr. W.B. YEATS: 'I think it is an insult to the national pride that this country should be asked to accept gifts from Canada while it refuses to give anything in return. It is, I think, an insult to the country to suggest that it is to be kept up by law and artificial barriers. The last Senator has described how in various parts of the world he found Irishmen occupying most important positions. These Irishmen should be able to occupy them at home without the law making a barrier to put them into them. If we do not pass this amendment we will have a precedent in this country for keeping out the experts from abroad whom we require and putting into position the ignoramuses at home whom we would be glad to lose. We will constantly have to import able men to teach this country many things that Irishmen had no possibility of acquiring. Every country in the position of this nation, at the beginning of its career, has to import talent. You are now to create a barrier which will make it impossible to do so, and, with the insulting theory that good intellects at home require protection. It is only the bad intellects at home that require protection, and I hope they will never get it.'

15th January, 1924. Irish Language

Mr. HAUGHTON: "I did not know until I looked up the Orders of the Day that I was to move this amendment. I saw the name, but I was not able to translate it…. I venture to suggest that it would be more consistent to give us the option of calling them Gárda Síochána or Civic Guards."

Mr. YEATS: 'The question troubles me very much. If I am attacked by a footpad and wish for protection how can I call for that protection by using words that I cannot pronounce?'

15th January, 1924. Saorstat Representation at British Empire Exhibition

Mr. YEATS: 'There is a certain body interested in artists, of which I am Chairman, and we had this matter before us at the last meeting, and there was exactly the same difference of opinion there as we find here now. We found out that invitations from the exhibition reached various artists at the end of last September to send in their work. We have been carrying on some correspondence with Ministers to find out whether the work of Irish artists would be classified with the general mass of English artists and other artists from different parts of the Empire, or whether they would be treated separately, and exhibited in a different room. I do not know whether we have had any satisfactory answer yet. It is possible it is too late to have them separated in a separate room, and that they would go along with others from different parts of the Empire under the head of "British Artists." If they went into a separate room we would have very distinct possibility for Ireland. About 16 years ago Sir Hugh Lane gave an exhibition of Irish Art in London, and it was discovered that some of the most famous artists were Irish. If our artists now had not the opportunity of exhibiting separately they would be driven back in the public estimation. At the same time we were not sure but it might be too late now to organise a separate Irish art section, and to bring into it men like Orpen and Lavery and Shannon, and if we could not recover these men we would have an Irish section that would not fully represent us. I am very much in favour of having Ireland represented at an Empire exhibition, but I am very anxious that the representation should be adequate, and I confess I have not before me any facts upon which I could feel assured upon that subject.'

23rd January, 1924. Public Safety (Powers of Arrest and Detention) Temporary Bill

Mr Yeats: "Providing for the inspection of such prisons, camps and other places, and the visiting of persons detained therein, by responsible persons, to be appointed by the Minister."

6th February, 1924. Courts of Justice Bill (Third Stage)

Mr. Yeats: 'I have not spoken hitherto on this Bill though I have voted in favour of the amendment of Senator Brown. What I rise for is to point out, to the President, a point of view which has occurred to me. Some of us so far from being hostile to the Government are deeply influenced by sympathy for the Government. We feel it has acted with great courage and justice in difficult times. We are scrupulously anxious to put aside our question of sympathy in favour of the question of judging these amendments. We want to judge these amendments in an abstract way, in the light of history, keeping in mind the fact that all civilised Governments that we know of, have found it necessary to insure the independence of the Judges from the Executive. It is difficult for us to press that point because we have felt that the Government have no desire to influence the decision of the judges. There is a feeling in this country among a number of people—it may be an unjust feeling—that the judges have hitherto been subservient to an alien Executive. Some members of this House have gone to the other end of the balance and thought that they would secure safety by being quite sure that an Irish Executive would have considerable control over judges. Those who take my point of view have done their best to secure that the Irish Judges shall be independent of every Executive whatsoever.'

19th March, 1924. Ministers and Secretaries Bill - The National Gallery

Mr. YEATS: 'I am troubled by one statement. The only matter in this Bill that interests me very much is the National Gallery and the Museum. I understand from the Attorney-General that if the Government has no policy for any particular Department it will not keep it within the purview of the Executive Council, or within the purview of Ministers within the Executive Council. If, therefore, the Government has no policy with regard to the National Gallery or the Museum, will it hand them over to the Minister for Fisheries to be administered by him, or by the Minister for Agriculture, as they were before, or by the Postmaster-General?'

19th March, 1924. Ministers and Secretaries Bill

The Earl of Mayo requires Ministers to provide written answers to representative's questions.

Mr Yeats: 'I hope, therefore, that the Government will absolutely refuse to answer any questions on anything whatsoever.'

3rd April, 1924. Ministers and Secretaries Bill

Dr. YEATS: 'With the indulgence of the Seanad I would like to say certain things that, properly speaking, I should have said on the Second Reading, but which I did not say for reasons which I will explain presently. At various periods during the last six months some persons interested in the National Gallery and the School of Art urged upon Ministers the desirability of placing the Museum, the National Gallery and the School of Art under the Ministry of Education. When this Bill came to the Seanad I saw with great satisfaction that these institutions were placed under the Ministry of Education. After the Second Reading I read the Bill with more attention, and I found that the Government possesses the right to transfer any particular institution to any particular Ministry it likes. That fills me with alarm. It is, no doubt, quite right that the Government should have such power, but I will take this opportunity of saying that I hope the Government will not transfer these particular institutions to any Ministry except the Ministry of Education, without consulting these bodies.

A number of us went on a deputation to one of the Ministers about five months ago. I have been trying to remember for the last half hour what Minister. I think it was the Minister for Industry and Commerce, but I cannot remember. The deputation laid before the Minister a very strong case, I think, to have these institutions included under the Ministry of Education. I would like to touch lightly on that now, because if the Government decide to transfer these institutions to some other branch nothing will be done but to lay on the Table of the Seanad certain papers announcing the fact. I may be away and may not see them, and other members of these bodies may know nothing about the matter. It is very important for the future industrial prosperity of this country that Art teaching should be brought into relationship to industry. That can only be done by some unified system of teaching which will include such institutions as the School of Art and the schools of the country. In the newer Universities in Germany and in Scandinavia they have professors of the arts for purely industrial reasons. They have found it essential in order to hold their own in the manufactory of the world that they should teach certain principles of good taste in order that their various forms of manufacture may possess good taste.

I begin with an example of what I hope may happen in this country. I understand that the Ministry of Education will form in the immediate future a Technical Board. One of the things that might very well come before that Technical Board for consideration is the lace industry of Ireland. If you go back a few years you will find that Ireland had an exceedingly prosperous lace industry, which employed a large number of people. That lace industry has lost its market to a very great extent, party through the hasty production of good old designs—the rough and ready manufacture at a quick rate of good old designs—and partly through the equally hasty production of exceedingly bad modern designs. For instance, I understand that in some cases 3s. 6d. would be given for a design to some student. That is about the same amount as the Free State Government thinks it necessary, I understand, to give for a design for a postage stamp. It would be possible for the Technical Board of the Ministry of Education to obtain from Austria or Sweden a teacher of lace-making, one with the highest possible accomplishments in the art, so that the industry might be restored to prosperity. Such a teacher would be employed in two ways, going to the country to inspect, and teaching at the School of Art. You have another example of the effect of teaching in the School of Art on the industries of this country. About twenty years ago, and I had a little to do with it, a teacher of stained glass was brought from England and employed in the Dublin School of Art. That teacher was brought chiefly through the efforts of Miss Purser. The manufacture of stained glass in Ireland was then the worst in the world. Now, some of the very best stained glass in the world is made here. One of the makers of the worst stained glass in the world twenty years ago was a man named Clarke. The maker of some of the best stained glass in the world to-day is his son. These are unusual topics to raise in the Seanad.'

AN CATHAOIRLEACH: 'I was about to intervene and say that myself, although I am very loth to curtail you as you are very interesting. What has this to do with the Ministers and Secretaries Bill?'

Dr. YEATS: 'I want the Government to keep Art teaching under the Ministry of Education in order that a unified system of Art teaching may arise in this country associated with education, so as to help manufactures. The deputation to the Minister was told that the argument against having the art institutions under the Ministry of Education was that they might be subordinate to a purely mechanical system of teaching, and thereby suffer as art institutions—I think that is very unlikely under the present Minister. That argument was put strongly. I beg the Government if they detach these institutions from the Ministry of Education, not to give them to any other Ministry, but to give them a Ministry of their own. The Arts in Ireland have suffered for several generations from having been under the Department of Agriculture. The Department of Agriculture had no policy in connection with them except a deadly one. When Sir Hugh Lane, for instance, was rejected when he applied for the position of head of the Museum in Dublin—the one great connoisseur we had—he was rejected on grounds which had nothing whatever to do with the Arts, but which were simply matters of policy of that Department. When the Department was remonstrated with, an official used this argument: "The time has not come to encourage the Arts in Ireland." If you place these particular institutions under any Ministry except the Ministry of Education or under a Ministry of their own, you will find that the time has not come to encourage the Arts in Ireland.'

Question—"That the Bill do now pass"—put and agreed to.

1st May, 1924. Report on Temporary Accommodation of the Oireachtas

Dr. YEATS: 'Senator Jameson said in the course of his speech that the great stones were being taken down from the Four Courts. If that is true, there may be some explanation of it. It is possible that the building is unsafe, and so on, but it is a matter so serious that I think, as the stones are being taken down, the Government should give some explanation to the public. We have there a building of great importance and great dignity, which we ought to have looked upon as a trust received from the past. It has been, unfortunately, almost destroyed, although not absolutely, I think, beyond the possibility of rebuilding, and I think we should preserve what remains of it. I desire to support what Senator Jameson has said.

The explanation of the curious position in which we find ourselves is that the majority of the Dáil think that the only thing for them to do is to go into Leinster House, but they think it would be an unlucky decision to make for themselves; and the Government would like to go into Kilmainham, but they think that it would be an unlucky decision to make for themselves, and both bodies of men are trying to get somebody else to make the decision. I read in Fraser's *Golden Bough* that there was a certain nation of antiquity which once a year used to launch a small model ship and sail out into the ocean and put on board all the reluctant community. If we do not do that we must make a deposit of the ill-luck of the community. The Joint Committee of both Houses has been appointed to act in the capacity of that model ship and carry away that ill-luck from the majority of the Dáil and the Government. I hope at this moment the Chairman is trying to exercise his ingenuity in framing a resolution to defeat that object.'

21st May, 1924. Future Business

Dr. YEATS: I wish to support one part of Senator Brown's speech. This House should remain sitting after the 4th July. There are certain Bills of pressing importance to this country. It is important we should not create a precedent of hasty legislation. If we create that precedent, it will last long after our time, but there is an immediate necessity for certain Bills. I am only speaking to draw the attention of the Government to the fact that no Bill has been introduced on copyright. I would like to draw the attention of the President to the fact that the copyright of certain Irish dramatists in America is being lost because there is no Copyright Act to enable the registration of those copyrights in Washington. I would, therefore, urge this House to remain sitting until we have passed the necessary legislation in order that the Government may find, when it meets in October, that our work has been done.

4th June, 1924 Peril to National Museum from Fire

'If, as a result of the Seanad staying here there was a fire, and the Irish gold ornaments and other national treasures were destroyed, it would be a final touch to the evil reputation of this nation. Certainly, I do not think that the Seanad could throw off responsibility on the question.'

4th June, 1924 Final Report of Committee on Irish Manuscripts

Dr. YEATS: 'I beg to move the adoption of the final Report of Committee on Irish Manuscripts as follows:—

Do ceapadh an Coiste seo do réir an Rúin seo leanas do cuireadh i bhfeidhm ag an Seanad ar an 19adh Aibreán, 1923:—

Coiste do cheapadh chun scéim do chur os comhair an Rialtais chun Láimhscribhínnibh Gaedhilge atá 'n-a luighe anois san Acadamh agus i gColáiste na Tríonóide agus i n-áiteannaibh eile nach iad do chur i n-eagair, do chlárú agus do chur amach; chun na canamhaintí beódha d'iniúchadh go cruinn is go beacht; chun foclóir foghanta na sean-Gaedhilge do chur le chéile is do chlóbhuail. Go mbheadh comhacht ag an gCoiste cabhair a d'iarraidh ó dhaoinibh nach baill de'n Seanad agus fiadhnais do thógaint 'n-a thaobh; na Seanadóirí seo do bheith ar an gCoiste sin:—Liam Yeats, Eilís Bean de Graoin, Eibhlín Bean Mhic Coisdealbha agus Eamonn MacGiollaiasachta; beirt mar líon-chomhairle.

Do réir an Rúin seo do tháinig an Coiste le chéile 26° Aibreán, 1° Bealtaine, 3° Bealtaine, 8° Bealtaine, 31 Bealtaine, 27° Meitheamh, 1923 agus 21° Bealtaine 1924.

Do héisteadh fianaise o sna finnithe seo leanas:—Dr. R.L. Praegar, Dr. R.I. Best, An Dr. Oir. O Leathlobhair, An Dr. Dubhglas de hIde, E.S. Mac Fhinn, F.T.C.D., An tOllamh Osborn O hAimhirgín, An tOllamh, Tomás O Raithile, Riseárd O Foghludha agus an tOllamh Tomás O Máille.

Do beartuíodh an socrú so leanas do mhola don tSeanaid:—

'This Committee was appointed by Resolution of the Seanad adopted on the 19th April, 1923, in the following terms:—

That a Committee of the Seanad be appointed to submit to the Government a scheme for the editing, indexing, and publishing of manuscripts in the Irish language, now lying in the Royal Irish Academy, Trinity College, and elsewhere; for the scientific investigation of the living dialects; for the compiling and publishing of an adequate dictionary of the older language. That the Committee have power to invite the assistance of persons not members of the Seanad and to take evidence on the subject; the Committee to consist of Senators W.B. Yeats, Mrs. Alice Stopford Green, Mrs. Costello, and Edward MacLysaght; two to form a quorum.

The Committee met in accordance with this Resolution on 26th April, 1st May, 3rd May, 31st May and 27th June, 1923, and on the 21st of May, 1924.

Evidence was heard from the following witnesses:—Dr. R.L. Praegar, Dr. R.I. Best, The Rev. Dr. Lawlor, Dr. Douglas Hyde, Mr. E.J. Gwynn, F.T.C.D.; Professor O'Bergin, Professor T. O'Rahilly, Mr. R. Foley, and Professor Tomás O'Máille.

It was decided to make the following report to the Seanad:—

Your Committee is gravely impressed by the responsibility now laid upon the Saorstát towards the Irish people. For the first time in many centuries our country, free and independent, is charged with the pious duty of preserving and making accessible to Irishmen the mass of learning and tradition which forms the basis of our National history—a body of manuscript tradition bequeathed to us by a noble succession of scholars and scribes throughout a thousand years of labour, and further enriched by folk-lore, folk-song and music, and the important study of topography.

It is well known that the British Government by its political and administrative policy through a long course of centuries did in fact make wreckage of Irish learning and language. But we are bound to remember that in our own time among the rulers there were men who did not remain deaf to claims of scholarship. We may recall the valuable services rendered from time to time by enlightened statesmen in funds allotted to such work as the Irish volumes of the "Rolls Series"; the "Historical Manuscripts Commission"; the "Ancient Laws of Ireland"; published by the Government under the direction of the Commissioners; the "Ulster Annals," which it published under direction of the Royal Irish Academy. The Government was prepared to do the same with the "Annals of Tigernach," when, unfortunately, the editor recommended died. A grant in aid to the Academy was employed, to issue the Todd Lectures, Facsimiles, etc., etc. For some years a grant was also given to the School of Irish Learning founded by Dr. Kuno Meyer, £700 in all.

These are a few illustrations of obligations to the country recognised by a British administration. We claim that the Irish Nation should fare no worse under a home Government, when it depends on its own honour, its own patriotism and resources, to complete the task of research, to preserve for future generations all that has been or can be saved of older learning, and to secure to the people of Ireland their full national tradition.

We may observe that the present moment is usually favourable for reviving and enlarging the study of Old Irish Law and government even beyond the bounds of this country; since the important research work of Professor MacNeill is rousing amongst foremost Continental scholars a new interest not only in questions of language but of the study of Comparative Law. By judicious use of its scholars and its means Ireland may take the lead in a new historic movement.

Your Committee, in the course of enquiry, has interviewed many witnesses of the most diverse groups and opinions. We have endeavoured to find out the points on which there is practically unanimous opinion, and to advise measures which are of urgent necessity, and promise useful results under conditions of sound administration and sympathetic aid. We therefore recommend the following suggestions as a basis for any scheme of financial assistance:—

(1) The editing and publishing of important texts, both of the early and the classical periods and of modern times, considering Irish literature as forming one indivisible whole. This work would involve grants in aid of publication to competent scholars.

(2) Publication of photographic facsimiles of important Codexes by the latest scientific processes. This is most essential for purposes of study. A grant to aid in the production of such a facsimile might be given to a learned body outside Ireland—for example, to the Oxford Press for the publication of Ms. Laud.

(3) The dictionary of Old Irish in course of preparation by the Royal Irish Academy under the editorship of Dr. Bergin—a work of enormous labour and difficulty—should receive further aid. Its progress must be slow, as the meaning and use of old Irish words can only be determined when more texts are made available by editors and photographers for the work of the Dictionary. At present three workers are employed, necessarily on half-time which is as much as the excessive strain of the task will allow. The number of workers might be increased to six—all on half-time.

(4) The publication of Catalogues of MSS. is of great importance for students. Catalogues should be compiled not only for the Royal Irish Academy but for collections elsewhere, as for example, in the Franciscan Convent, and the King's Inns, the National Library, and many others in Ireland or outside. We suggest that the Dictionary workers, and others, now employed at half-time, might most profitably also serve in this task of cataloguing.

(5) Investigation of living dialects. This work is of immense importance when dialects are rapidly dying out. It has been done in patches of the Irish speaking regions, but a systematic study is in fact essential, and the work cannot be relegated to volunteers. Research should be endowed. For example, a grant to a trained phonetist would be of the utmost value, with aid in the publication of his results. It is unnecessary to add how great would be the stimulus given by such training to local workers in Gaelic-speaking regions.

(6) Folk-lore, songs and traditions cannot be neglected. The best aid would be a grant towards publication of work done, as for example, a grant to the Irish-Folk Song Society in aid of publishing work submitted by the Society and approved.

(7) The Academy has drawn attention to two other needs of a pressing character: a survey of the antiquities of the country, such as is at present being carried out by Commissions in England, Wales and Scotland. In this connection it remarks that the measurements and plans of earthworks of different types and surveys of cairns already published by the Academy would serve as a nucleus for this undertaking. The work might be very gradually carried out, district by district.

Excavations should also be conducted under scientific direction of the more important archæological sites, to determine their age, significance and historical associations.

In the view of the Committee all grants should be allocated by an authoritative body, including trained Irish scholars, animated with the desire to encourage students by the assurance of means of publication of their work. We have, therefore, enquired into the best machinery by which these suggestions may profitably be carried out, and the body to which public funds should be entrusted.

The body which in our opinion is marked out for the development of Irish studies is the "Royal Irish Academy," which has now incorporated the "School of Irish Learning."

The Academy was founded to encourage learning in a wide range of Sciences in which it has earned distinction. It has also charge of linguistics and archaeology, and Irish research has long been a notable part of its business. Since it has no special funds for archaeological work, apart from occasional grants, its resources have been spent on publication. The Government grant is £1,600, and £885 comes from members' subscriptions and other sources. On a total income of £2,485 —

with establishment charges of £1,050—the Academy shows an admirable record of careful administration. It must be remembered that the benefits it contributes to Irish learning include a library rich in Irish books, to which the public have admission; a valuable collection of ancient MSS.; and also the printing in its "Proceedings" of important Irish communications. For many years past an average of six hundred pounds—over a third of its annual income available for general publication —has been expended on Irish subjects, literature, archaeology and the like. At the moment the Leabhar na hUidhre (Book of the Dun Cow) is being published at a cost of about £1,000. The task of publishing the Irish Dictionary, now calculated at nearly £600 a year, must necessarily occupy many years, and remain a heavy charge on finances. All strictly Irish work of the Academy is delegated to an "Irish Studies Committee," drawn from two older groups —the Dictionary Committee and the Irish Manuscripts Committee. It has enlisted in its service all the best Irish scholars, whose knowledge, experience, and ardour in the cause cannot be surpassed.

The "School of Irish Learning" was founded in 1903 by Dr. Kuno Meyer at a time when there was no regular teaching in Dublin of an advanced nature in Old or Middle Irish. The School held summer courses by professors invited to lecture from England, Scotland, Germany, Denmark, and Norway, and students were attracted from oversea by the remarkable training thus offered. Travelling scholarships were also given by the School with excellent results. With a single exception all the professors and lecturers in Irish in the National University Colleges have been students of the School, as also have been Professors of Celtic in Great Britain and abroad. The work of the School has for some years past been limited to summer courses, the last of which, in 1923, was a remarkable course in Phonetics, and the study of a living Irish dialect by Professor Sommerfelt, of Christiania.

An important and enduring work of the School was its journal *Eriu*, devoted to Irish philology and literature, and recognised in the learned world as the leading review of its kind. The School also published textbooks on Old and Modern Irish which are now used by scholars in every country.

It was felt desirable at this time to unite forces working for Irish scholarship, so as to avoid all overlapping of effort, all conceivable competition in publications, and all unnecessary doubling of rent and services. An amicable arrangement has, therefore, been made by which the School of Irish Learning has been incorporated in the Academy, and so far as Irish studies are concerned, *Eriu* remains the common Journal, the representative work of the united body.

Your Committee, therefore, after careful consideration, recommend that the authoritative financial control of any grant allotted by the Government should be placed in the Academy whose Irish Committee is fully qualified, trained in this special work, generous in outlook, and easy of access to all.

We believe that additional funds allotted to it by the Government will be spent not only with a due sense of stewardship, but with an earnest desire to advance the cause of Irish Learning, and to complete the national work of restoring to the Irish people their inherited tradition both of ancient and of later times.

We fully realise the overwhelming claims on the Government in these times. On the other hand we feel it to be of great importance that some earnest should at once be given of its sympathy with the national desire to renew and broaden its historical tradition and faith. We, therefore, recommend that an additional annual grant be given to the Academy, and especially earmarked for the disposal of the Committee of Irish studies on the lines indicated in this Report. In the existing state of our national finances we do not name a definite sum, but we urge that as liberal a grant as possible should be given immediately, and that the Government should bear in mind that as soon as our financial position allows not less than £5,000 per annum should be devoted to Irish research.

(Sighnithe),

W.B. YEATS, Cathaoirleach an Choiste (Chairman of the Committee).

EIBHLIN BEAN MAC COISDEALBHA.

A.S. GREEN.

EAMON MAC GIOLLAIASACHTA.'

I hope and indeed I have no doubt that the Seanad will accept this report. I would like, however, to draw the special attention of one section in the Seanad to the nature of the report. Certain members of the Seanad have. I think, a great dislike to pray in a language they do not understand. There are other members of the Seanad who dislike having our Acts of Parliament expensively printed in two languages. That may be right or wrong; but this is an entirely different question. We are asking the Seanad to urge upon the Government to do a work for learning, a work for literature and a work for history which any Government in the world would consider its duty and its privilege. This country possesses a great mass of old mediaeval literature in the Irish language. There are great collections of manuscripts in the Royal Irish Academy in the Library of Trinity College, at Maynooth, and in the Franciscan library. There are very large collections of manuscripts in other countries. There is a great collection in the British Museum, in the Bodlean, and in the Louvain. These manuscripts are a historical trust to this nation, but they should be interpreted, edited, indexed, and catalogued.

Much work has been done on them in the past — much by Irishmen, much by Germans, and to some extent we may say that the centre of Irish scholarship has in recent years been in Germany. But the German interest is only primarily a philological interest. If we are to exhaust the value of these manuscripts for literature and history we must do that work ourselves. They possess first of all their value to this country; then they possess their value to the world. They consist of stories, annals, and poetry. I think that all the famous stories have been translated and have been edited. We will learn nothing new of importance about Finn and Cuchulain and other old Irish heroes or Kings of the legendary period. The annals have to a great extent been edited and translated, but I understand, they have been badly edited and translated in many cases, and if they are to be of historical value that work has to be done over again. In the case of poetry there is probably still a large quantity of untranslated and of even unread poetry.

That poetry would be of two kinds: First of all, what is called the official poetry, not of great literary value but of great historical value — the work of the official Bards. But there is also much poetry which is personal expression — that kind of poetry which Dr. Kuno Meyer has translated in recent years. If we can judge the unread and unedited by the read and edited, they will be of supreme value. I should say that we had evidence given before us, that great scholars might work for 100 years on the old Irish manuscripts now in the possession of the Nation, and in the possession of other nations without having exhausted the subject. We are anxious that provision should be made for that work and that the work should be carried out. Already the traditional imagination in these old books has had a powerful effect upon the life, and I may say upon the politics, of Ireland. People forget that the twenties, forties and fifties of the last century was the forming period of Irish nationality, and that the work was begun by O'Donovan, Petrie and men steeped in this old literature.

We owe it also to learning and the scholarship of the world that we should provide means for the doing of this great work. Twenty years ago, in Paris, I knew slightly the great French scholar, D'Arbois de Jubanville, who devoted his life to the study of our literature because he believed that only through that literature could he find light on the most important secular event in human history. Going back 1,000 or 1,200 years before Christ we find Dorian tribes descending on the Mediterranean civilization. They destroyed much and wandered much, and it has been held that we owe to their destruction, the story, of the Fall of Troy, and to their wandering, the Story of Odyssey. D'Arbois de Jubanville considered that only through Irish literature can you rediscover the civilization of these tribes before they entered the Mediterranean. That does not mean than our people were the Greeks or that our literature is as old as 1,200 years before Christ, but our legends and our books have preserved and gathered together the old literature and much of the history of a similar period. We ask you to urge upon the Government that they, shall place in the hands of the Royal Irish Academy sufficient funds. We heard much evidence and we came to the conclusion that the Royal Irish Academy itself contains within its limits practically all the great Irish scholars and that it is the proper body to carry out this work in a spirit of scholarship. The danger is that it may be carried out in some other spirit. It is most important that nothing should be taken into consideration except the interest of scholarship alone.

It should not be allowed to become a means by which some man will make a living until he gets some other occupation; the money should be used to help a man whose life-work is study and scholarship. It has been contended that the Royal Irish Academy is not a democratic body and that therefore we should not ask the Government to endow it in this way. I have heard it contended that it is not a democratic body because by its rules it can only elect seven new members every year. Twenty years ago I should not have been able to invite you, with the same confidence, to ask the Royal Irish Academy to undertake this work, because twenty years ago it had not that rule. It could elect any person who professed himself interested in the subjects with which it dealt. That rule of electing only seven members a year was instituted in order to raise the position of the Academy by making it necessary to elect those only who were eminent in the studies of the Academy, and not merely interested in those studies. I think I am right in saying that since that rule was passed the Academy has risen more and more in the estimation of the learned, and in helping it to do its work we are helping a body which has advanced the learning of this country. I beg to move the adoption of the Report.'

19th June, 1924. Temporary accommodation of the Oireachtas

Dr. YEATS: 'I move:—

That the consideration of this Report be postponed for a fortnight.

I do this because it recommends that the Parliament should remain in the present building. We are very anxious to have some investigation made as to whether the Museum is safe from fire, and I do not think we can very well consider the matter until we have had some investigation. Some of us are going, in the course of a few minutes, to see the Minister on the question, and I think it may be desirable to have a Special Committee of this House appointed to take expert advice. I do not see how we can come to any conclusion on the question at all until we can have some evidence before us as to the security or otherwise of the national treasures. I, therefore, move that the consideration of the Report be postponed for a fortnight.'

Dr. YEATS: 'I simply want to say, as a matter of explanation, that I have brought forward this resolution with no other object whatever, except to find out whether the collections are or are not in danger from fire or otherwise from our residence here. I have not done this in the interest of the Royal Dublin Society or because of preference for any particular site. But I do think we have got to find out, and the responsibility is ours individually, whether our residence here is causing danger to the national collections. I think the Chairman has made our case in telling us that it was not raised until a few weeks ago, in other words, that it was not considered by the Committee.'

Dr. YEATS: 'Another question I would like to have asked the Board of Works as to the protection against fire is, whether they had to improve this protection at the instance of Senator Mrs. Green's agitation. Had they to have more protection or to improve it, because if they improved it, then the former protections were inadequate, and the Board of Works are in the dock. I see every reason for postponing this matter until we get expert opinion. I am only asking for postponement, not rejection of the Report. It is quite possible that when we have heard this opinion we will decide that this is the best place. I do not know——' Motion agreed.

2nd July, 1924. Railways Bill 1924, Third Stage

Dr. YEATS: 'The last time I spoke in the Seanad was on a question connected with Gaelic. It was to bring before the Seanad a report of a committee that had been dealing with Gaelic studies. I asked the Seanad to support a proposal by which the Government would be asked to give £5,000 for the endowment of Gaelic. Senator Colonel Moore tells me that he hopes to get the Government to endow Gaelic. If such a proposal comes before the Seanad, I will certainly support it. I ask the Seanad to throw out this amendment. I do so in the interests of the sincerity of Irish intellect, and not in the interests of those who pretend that they know a language that they do not know.'

Mr. MacLYSAGHT: I did not say that you know Irish.

Dr. YEATS: 'I have tried to learn it. When you put up, as this amendment proposes, a notice telling a man where he is to cross a railway line, you put it up to give him the best practical information. That is the only thing you have to consider. To put that up in the Irish language is to create a form of insincerity that is injurious to the general intellect and thought of this country, and to create an irritation against the Gaelic language. That causes a general irritation against all Irish thought, all Irish feeling, and all Irish propaganda. That is a cause of irritation that is increasing daily in this country, I am sorry to say. If the Gaelic League or any other Irish national interest is injured it will be injured by an attempt to force Irish on those who do not want it. Endow creation by scholarships, and press that on the Government, but do not set up a pretence of people knowing a language that they do not know by perpetually printing, and in other ways, exhibiting something in the Irish language.'

Amendment withdrawn

3rd July, 1924. Finance Bill, 1924: Second Stage

Dr. YEATS: 'I am not competent to give an opinion on the great issue of Protection versus Free Trade. The Government, however, is engaged in certain experimental measures, and that justifies me in bringing before them one particular industry in this country. When the Fiscal Committee was meeting various persons, engaged in the making of stained glass, brought before them a proposal that they should get Protection. I shall deal in a moment with the argument why they need that protection. I think the Fiscal Committee, or certainly some of its members, were exceedingly sympathetic towards that proposal, but as the Committee decided to report in favour of Free Trade they were unable to put anything in the Report on the subject. The position of the stained-glass industry in Ireland is this: It is purchasing now some of the very best glass in the world and it has been faced for some years past, except one short interval, with the competition of the most inferior stained-glass which is produced in Germany for Irish use, especially produced for the bad taste of Ireland. It is impossible that our stained-glass can compete against the mass production of Europe. Under no circumstances whatever can it do so, because an artist producing fine glass cannot supervise more than a very limited number of assistants. The moment you increase those assistants beyond a certain point, the quality of that glass and the design deteriorates. You cannot get the same qualities of colour. The mass manufacture of glass will always be inferior. There was a short period during the war when our Irish stained-glass had not to face that competition. They at once found an exceedingly fine market at home, and it was the finding of that exceedingly fine market which helped them to establish them in their great artistic pre-eminence as creators of that beautiful glass. Then, with the Armistice came the old competition of Germany in a much worse form, but owing to the depreciation of the German coinage, the Germans were able to import their glass much cheaper than ever before.

I do not ask the Government to put on such a tariff as would exclude German glass produced under these circumstances. They would have to put on an absolutely prohibitive tariff, probably 300 per cent., but I would ask the Government to consider the advisability of putting a tax of say 50 per cent. on German glass, until the money market becomes normal between England, Ireland and Germany. Nobody connected with the production of glass in Ireland desires to have a tax against English glass. I think I am right in saying that there is not one person in Ireland connected with the making of glass that desires such a tax. The reason of that is that they are artists, not manufacturers. They recognise that Ireland and

England are now producing the best glass in the world, and that it would be an unfair thing for Ireland to seek an economic advantage against English glass. They believe that it would be to the advantage of this country, and its reputation. if the Government were to protect it against the very inferior quality and products of other countries that are made to be consumed in this country and this country only. It requires a firm Government to say certain things are fine and certain things are not fine and should not be encouraged. The Government has shown great courage in many ways and I suggest it should show enough courage to support what is fine in the arts.'

16th July, 1924. Temporary Accommodation of the Oireachtas

Mr. YEATS: 'My interest in this question is almost entirely confined to seeing to it that the contents of the Museum are safe. I do not know whether the members of the Dáil or all the Senators realise that practically no Museum is insured, that the contents of Museums are so valuable that money cannot replace these articles. The National Gallery in London, the great museum in South Kensington, and the British Museum or the Irish Museum are not insured. You must, therefore, see to the safety of the Museum in the way that you do not see to the safety of any ordinary building. Furthermore, you cannot trust merely to your fire-extinguishing apparatus— though in museums that is generally of the most perfect kind—because the water hose may do as much injury as the fire to the Museum. There is only one thing that you can do with the Museum, and that is to see to it that no fire can break out in it. Certain precautions are taken all over the world. In no museum in the world is smoking permitted. Now, here we have a refreshment room where there is cooking. In museums where there is a refreshment room they are specially constructed on concrete floors, so that fire cannot break out. Furthermore, all these museums of any importance are detached buildings. About twenty years ago it was discovered that the National Gallery in London had an inflammable building up against it. There was great agitation in England, and there was great indignation, and that building was pulled down. In the Bodleian Library, which I know very well—I used it for several years—artificial light is not permitted, because it is an old inflammable building, though not more inflammable than our building. These are the ordinary precautions taken all over the world for the protection of national treasures. Are we going to be less civilised than any other country?

Some few weeks ago the various persons whose business it was to look after these treasures memorialised the Government in various forms. The

Royal Irish Academy laid weighty evidence before the Government to show that the national treasures were not safe. The Visitors to the Museum, who are persons appointed under Act of Parliament to take care of the treasures there, laid a memorial before the Government, showing that the national treasures were not safe. A petition was laid before the Government signed by bishops, peers, representatives of all the learned institutions of Ireland, and some twenty Senators of this House, stating that the national treasures were not safe. The answer to that was the statement by the Government that they were safe. Then, some three weeks ago we postponed the report of the Special Committee that we might see the technical evidence upon which the Government had stated that the national treasures were safe. I have here on the Table, where it should have been laid by the Government, the report of the technical advisers. It was sent to the Clerk of this House that members might see it. I will read you one extract from the letter written on the 22nd June by the Board of Works to the President's Secretary:—

"We beg to report that the danger of fire to the National Museum is undoubtedly increased by the fact that the Seanad and its officials are housed there, and that Senators and officials are accustomed to smoke on the premises. It is also true that the annexes of the Museum at present used as refreshment rooms and kitchen are lined with wood, and are very inflammable, and that there is a wooden hut near the annexe occupied by soldiers, which also is of an inflammable nature."

And yet we are told the national treasures are safe! The Board of Works might have said more. They might have pointed out that the floors are of wood, that the centre of danger —the kitchen and the bar—are flanked by rooms containing highly inflammable material. Any of you can go and look at the place next the dining-room and you will find a room packed with inflammable show-cases. If you go into the passage in the same building you will find bottles full of spirits —not the spirits they have in the bar, but spirits in another form equally dangerous in case of fire. Then the Board of Works, in this letter which I have here, go on to say:

"Special precautions have been and are being taken to meet these risks."

They define their precautions. They are putting up a fireproof door between the passage and these buildings. They are putting up a fireproof door between the building on that side and the other Museum. They are putting up a further fireproof door above the way that leads down to the spirit store, which is under the kitchen. Then they go on to say that there are other precautions. There is, they say, a fireproof door outside the room upstairs where the gold ornaments are housed. There is no fireproof door there. There is a burglar-proof door.

They say an inspector goes round every night and that that is the best precaution of all. If that is the best precaution of all, I think very badly of the others. If that man does his work properly it will take him at least an hour to see after the library which he is to inspect, and to see that all the windows there are properly shut. I am informed that it would take him several hours to make his rounds, if he does his work properly. A fire might therefore have a very considerable start before he discovered its existence. And that is the best precaution according to the Board of Works! Then, why were not those precautions taken months and months ago? Can we trust anything the Board of Works says to us when we have it that it is only now it takes such precautions. Is it a fitting guardian of the public treasures? The only thing it does, as a result of Mrs. Green's agitation, is to put up those fire-proof doors. If the Oireachtas remains here, there is only one thing to be done if the Museum is to be safe—that is to rebuild the kitchen and those other apartments somewhere else. The chief danger is from those buildings.

I cannot imagine that the Government desires to take less precaution in guarding its national treasures than Governments do in other countries. I can only think that the situation has arisen because of the extraordinary apathy of this country—an apathy that has come upon everything in connection with the national life in the recent past. I cannot imagine that if the mind of this country were what it was seven or eight years ago, the people would think for a moment of leaving in any greater danger their treasures than the treasures, say, in South Kensington Museum or the British Museum. These treasures are the only visible signs we have that we ever had a civilisation. I do not think that the Government, if they gave thought to the matter, would like to set such an example before the people of this country of contempt of things of the mind. They are bringing in an ambitious Education Bill. They talk occasionally of their desire to see this an able, intellectual country. But if they are going to pay less respect than any other country does to their national treasures, to the irreplaceable things, who in this country will take them seriously when they speak of their desire to see this country able and educated?'

Motion put and declared carried.

16th July, 1924. National Museum and Adjoining Buildings (Danger of Fire)

Mr. YEATS: 'I beg to move:—

That the Seanad is of opinion that for the purpose of satisfying the public mind as to the sufficiency of the safeguards provided against fire in the National Museum and the adjoining buildings, the Government should obtain a detailed report from an independent expert; and that inasmuch as Sir Edwin Lutyens will be in Dublin by invitation of the Tailteann Games Committee in August, he should be requested to make the report.

I do not think that the Board of Works would object to an independent expert being asked to give an opinion on this matter. I find in one of their statements this occurs: "If the Government were to ask to make a special inquiry into the matter, it would be desirable to agree to do so, and to appoint a committee for the purpose, as the report of such a committee would probably have more weight than Departmental representations." That statement of the Board of Works admits on principle the desirability of there being some outside report upon the question. I was in London until last night, when I returned for this meeting, and while there I inquired from various persons whose business was the safety of museums from fire, and I was told that Sir Edwin Lutyens would be the right person to examine into the question and to make an expert report. I went to him and asked him if he was invited by the Government to make a report, would he do so, and he said he certainly would. He will be in Dublin on August 1st as the guest of the nation. I think he would be regarded as the most acceptable person to do this. There is no one connected with architecture in the world who is a higher authority or whose word or opinion would be more universally accepted.'

Motion agreed.

17th October, 1924. Solution of Outstanding National Problems.

The Resolution is as follows:—

"That this Seanad is of opinion that the interests of the country as a whole would be best served by an agreed solution of outstanding problems affecting the relations between the Irish Free State and Northern Ireland."

Mr. YEATS: 'I do not think the Senator who has just spoken fully understands the resolution. We are not asking the Government to withdraw from the Commission, and we are not asking that the Commission should come to an end. We perfectly understand the Government's promise to those people. The Government promised those people the Treaty and they are bound to give the people of this country the Treaty; they cannot give anything else but the Treaty. What the resolution suggests is that before the Commission has reported, President Cosgrave, without giving anything away whatever, should make another appeal to the North to meet him in counsel. He is surrendering nothing. I think we quite recognise that nothing will probably come out of that appeal of President Cosgrave. To some extent we have to think of the future; we have to think of educating the next generation.

Results of a very evil kind may happen from the report of the Commission, no matter what way it reports, and it is exceedingly important that no responsibility for those results should lie with the Government of the Free State. I have no hope of seeing Ireland united in my time, or of seeing Ulster won in my time; but I believe it will be won in the end, and not because we fight it, but because we govern this country well. We can do that, if I may be permitted as an artist and a writer to say so, by creating a system of culture which will represent the whole of this country and which will draw the imagination of the young towards it.

Now, I have spoken very seriously but I want to turn from seriousness to a fact which has been burning in my imagination since this meeting began —a discovery I made which has lightened this serious subject for me. I have been looking for a historical precedent for the remarkable fact that certain Englishmen who afterwards became Cabinet Ministers and in other ways rose to the highest positions in the State went over to Ulster about 15 years ago and armed the people at a time of entire peace and urged them, and are now urging them, to use these arms against us. I have found a historical precedent which establishes that it is an old custom of the British Government. I have found that Edmund Burke in the middle of the eighteenth century drew attention to a very remarkable item in the

Estimates of the year. It was an item of so much money for the purchase of five gross of scalping knives, which scalping knives were intended to be given to the American Indians that they might scalp the French.'
Motion carried.

10th June, 1925. Shannon Electricity Bill 1925 Third Stage.

Dr. YEATS: 'There are many monuments which we should respect and which will become of great importance to this country, not only to the education of our own people, but to the tourists who come here. Therefore, they will be of financial value. There is a famous poem called "Clonmacnoise," which will be sung by the people of other countries. A poem of the late Mr. Rolleston is so beautiful that it will in all probability bring many tourists into that district if you can protect the ruins.

"In a quiet, watered land, a land of roses,

Stands St. Kieran's city fair,

And the warriors of Erin,

in their famous generations.

Slumber there."'

'I think I am the first person who has quoted a poem in the Seanad. I only do so because I am sure the poem will be, to use the appropriate words, "a definite asset."'

Colonel MOORE: 'I am not satisfied with the Minister's statement. It has to be done with the consent of the owner. I remember a few years ago when a certain person owned Tara, and certain people came over from England and they said the Ark of the Covenant was at Tara.''' They proceeded to dig up the whole place. Arthur Griffith went there and protested, but it was no use… There was much damage done to Tara. I would like something to be done in the case of unreasonable men of that kind, and so prevent them from destroying ancient monuments.'

Dr. YEATS: 'We stopped that man. I was on that expedition.'

11th June, 1925. Debate on Divorce Legislation

Dr. YEATS: 'I did not intend to be uncomplimentary. I should have said I do not intend to speak merely to the House. I have no doubt whatever, if circumstances were a little different, a very easy solution would be found for this whole difficulty. I judge from conversations that I have had with various persons that many would welcome a very simple solution, namely, that the Catholic members should remain absent when a Bill of Divorce was brought before the House that concerned Protestants and non-Catholics only, and that it would be left to the Protestant members, or some Committee appointed by those Protestant members, to be dealt with. I think it would be the first instinct of the members of both Houses to adopt some such solution and it is obvious, I think, that from every point of view of national policy and national reputation that would be a wise policy.

It is perhaps the deepest political passion with this nation that North and South be united into one nation. If it ever comes that North and South unite the North will not give up any liberty which she already possesses under her constitution. You will then have to grant to another people what you refuse to grant to those within your borders. If you show that this country, Southern Ireland, is going to be governed by Catholic ideas and by Catholic ideas alone, you will never get the North. You will create an impassable barrier between South and North, and you will pass more and more Catholic laws, while the North will, gradually, assimilate its divorce and other laws to those of England. You will put a wedge into the midst of this nation. I do not think this House has ever made a more serious decision than the decision which, I believe, it is about to make on this question. You will not get the North if you impose on the minority what the minority consider to be oppressive legislation. I have no doubt whatever that in the next few years the minority will make it perfectly plain that it does consider it exceedingly oppressive legislation to deprive it of rights which it has held since the 17th century. These rights were won by the labours of John Milton and other great men, and won after strife, which is a famous part of the history of the Protestant people.

There is a reason why this country did not act upon what was its first impulse, and why this House and the Dáil did not act on their first impulse. Some of you may probably know that when the Committee was set up to draw up the Constitution of the Free State, it was urged to incorporate in the Constitution the indissolubility of marriage and refused to do so. That was the expression of the political mind of Ireland. You are now urged to act on the advice of men who do not express the political mind, but who express the religious mind. I admit it must be exceedingly difficult for members of this House to resist the pressure that has been brought upon them. In the long warfare of this country with England the Catholic clergy took the side of the people, and owing to that they possess here an influence that they do not possess anywhere else in Europe. It is difficult for you, and I am sure it is difficult for Senator Mrs. Wyse-Power, stalwart fighter as she is——'

Dr. YEATS: 'Addressing the Catholic Truth Society in October last he used these words:

"No power on earth can break the marriage bond until death ... that is true of all baptised persons no matter what the denomination may be. To be sure we hear that a section of our fellow-countrymen favour divorces. Well, with nothing but respect and sympathy for all our neighbours, we have to say that we place the marriages of such people higher than they do themselves. Their marriages are unbreakable before God and we cannot disobey God by helping to break them."

That is to say you are to legislate on purely theological grounds and you are to force your theology upon persons who are not of your religion. It is not a question of finding it legally difficult or impossible to grant to a minority what the majority does not wish for itself. You are to insist upon members of the Church of Ireland or members of no church taking a certain view of Biblical criticism, or of the authority of the text upon which that criticism is exercised, a view that they notoriously do not take. If you legislate upon such grounds there is no reason why you should stop there. There is no reason why you should not forbid civil marriages altogether seeing that civil marriage is not marriage in the eyes of the Church——'

Dr. YEATS: 'These are topics on which it is desirable that the use of words should be carefully weighed beforehand. That must be my excuse. It is just as much adultery according to that view as the remarriage of divorced persons is. Nor do I see why you should stop at that, for we teach in our schools and universities and print in our books many things which the Catholic Church does not approve of. Once you attempt legislation upon religious grounds you open the way for every kind of intolerance and for every kind of religious persecution. I am not certain that there are not people in this country who would not urge you on to that course. I have nothing but respect for Most Rev. Dr. O'Donnell. I am told that he is a vigorous and able man, and I can say this for the speech from which I quoted, that if unwise in substance it was courteous in form. But what have I to say of the following extract from an article by Father Peter Finlay:—

"The refusal to legalise divorce is no denial of justice to any section of our people; it is no infringement of the fullest civil and religious liberty which our Constitution guarantees to all. As well say that prohibition of suttee is a denial of justice to the Hindu widow. The Hindu widow had a far clearer right to do herself to death on her husband's funeral pyre—her religion imposed it upon her as a duty—than any member of a Christian community can have to put away his wife and enter into a state of public legalised adultery. England acted justly, and in fulfilment of a plain and grave moral obligation, when she forbade suttee in India. The Irish Free State will act justly, and in fulfilment of a plain and grave moral obligation, in refusing to legalise absolute divorce and re-marriage among ourselves."

In a previous part of the essay he compares divorce with polygamy, robbery and murder. I know little or nothing about Father Finlay's career. It may have been eminent and distinguished, but I am sure that very few members of this House will think with pleasure of following the guidance of a man who speaks with such monstrous discourtesy of a practice which has been adopted by the most civilised nations of the modern world—by Germany, England, America, France and Scandinavian countries. He must know that by every kind of statistics, by every standard except the narrowest, that those nations, because they so greatly exceed us in works, exceed us in virtue. Father Peter Finlay has been supported by an ecclesiastic of the Church of Ireland, the Bishop of Meath, who has even excelled him in invective. Perceiving, no doubt, that indissoluble marriage, which for the guilty party at least, he passionately desires, has in other countries made men and women exceedingly tolerant of certain forms of sexual immorality, he declares that every erring husband or erring wife should be treated as a robber, a forger, or a murderer. Now, there is one great difference between Father Finlay in his relation to this House and the Bishop of Meath. I think that Father Finlay may influence votes in this House, but I am sure that the Bishop of Meath has not influenced one. What is more, if the entire Protestant episcopacy in Ireland came out with a declaration on this subject, it would not influence a vote in this House. It is one of the glories of the Church in which I was born that we have put our Bishops in their places in discussions requiring legislation. Even in those discussions involving legislation on matters of religion they count only according to their individual intelligence and knowledge. The rights of divorce, and many other rights, were won by the Protestant communities in the teeth of the most bitter opposition from their clergy. The living, changing, advancing human mind, sooner or later refuses to accept this legislation from men who base their ideas on the interpretation of doubtful texts in the Gospels. It is necessary to say, and I say it without fear of contradiction, that there is not a scholar of eminence in Europe to-day who considers that the Gospels are, in the strict sense of the words, historical documents. Their importance is devotional, not historical. For any ecclesiastic to advice statesmen to base legislation on a passage that may lack historical validity, is to appeal to the ignorance of the people. I am sure that the majority of those who favour the indissolubility of marriage, are under the impression that it preserves sexual morality in the country that adopts it. I think that before they are entirely certain on that point, they should study the morality of countries where marriage is indissoluble,—Spain, Italy, and the South American nations. We are not proposing to take from those nations our economics, our agricultural or technical instruction, but we are proposing to take from them our marriage laws. Before doing so, I think it would be well to make some study of the effect of the marriage laws on those nations. I have gone to the authorities available, and I find that, on the whole, they have successfully suppressed much evidence of immorality. There are no reports in the newspapers of divorce proceedings. The usual number of children are born in wedlock, but I do find that there is a great uncertainty as to the parentage of these children, but then, public opinion discourages curiosity on that subject, and it is a habit to discourage any inquiry into the emotional relations of men and women among modern communities. This is a demand for happiness, which increases with education, and men and women who are held together against their will and reason soon cease to recognise any duty to one another.

You are going to have indissoluble marriage, but you are going to permit separation. You cannot help yourself there. You are going to permit young people who cannot live together, because of some intolerable wrong, to separate. You are going to invite men and women in the prime of life to accept for the rest of their existence the law of the cloisters. Do you think you are going to succeed in what the entire of Europe has failed to do for the last 2,000 years? Are you going to impose the law of the cloister on those young people? If not, you are not going to raise the morality of this country by indissoluble marriage. A great English judge, speaking out of the immensity of his experience, said that there is no cause of irregular sexual relations so potent as separation without the possibility of remarriage.

This is a question which I know to be exciting a good deal of interest. I know something of the opinions of those who will make the next generation in this country. I know it, perhaps, better than most members of this House, and I am going to give those young people, speaking from here, a piece of advice, though they are, perhaps, of a far less excitable temperament than I am. I urge them not to be unduly excited. There is no use quarrelling with icebergs in warm water. These questions will solve themselves. Father Peter Finlay and the Bishop of Meath will have their brief victory, but we can leave them to it.

I have said that this is a tolerant country, yet, remembering that we have in our principal streets certain monuments, I feel it necessary to say that it would be wiser if I had said this country is hesitating.

I have no doubt whatever that, when he iceberg melts it will become an exceedingly tolerant country. The monuments are on the whole encouraging. I am thinking of O'Connell, Parnell, and Nelson. We never had any trouble about O'Connell. It was said about O'Connell, in his own day, that you could not throw a stick over a workhouse wall without hitting one of his children, but he believed in the indissolubility of marriage, and when he died his heart was very properly preserved in Rome. I am not quite sure whether it was in a bronze or marble urn, but it is there, and I have no doubt the art of that urn was as bad as the other art of the period. We had a good deal of trouble about Parnell when he married a woman who became thereby Mrs. Parnell.'

Dr. YEATS: 'I am passing on. I would hate to leave the dead alone. When that happened, I can remember the Irish Catholic Bishops coming out with a declaration that he had thereby doubled his offence. That is, fundamentally, the difference between us. In the opinion of every Irish Protestant gentleman in this country he did what was essential as a man of honour. Now you are going to make that essential act impossible, and thereby affront an important minority of your countrymen. I am anxious to draw the attention of the Bishop of Meath to Nelson. There is a proposal to remove Nelson because he interferes with the traffic. Now, I would suggest to the Protestant Bishop of Meath that he should advocate the removal of Nelson on strictly moral grounds. We will then have the whole thing out, and discover whether the English people who teach the history of Nelson to their children, and hold it before the country as a patriotic ideal, or the Bishop of Meath represent, on the whole, public opinion. The Bishop of Meath would not, like his predecessors in Ireland eighty years ago, have given Nelson a Pillar. He would have preferred to give him a gallows, because Nelson should have been either hanged or transported. I think I have not greatly wronged the dead in suggesting that we have in our midst three very salutary objects of meditation which may, perhaps, make us a little more tolerant.

I wish to close more seriously; this is a matter of very great seriousness. I think it is tragic that within three years of this country gaining its independence we should be discussing a measure which a minority of this nation considers to be grossly oppressive. I am proud to consider myself a typical man of that minority. We against whom you have done this thing, are no petty people. We are one of the great stocks of Europe. We are the people of Burke; we are the people of Grattan; we are the people of Swift, the people of Emmet, the people of Parnell. We have created the most of the modern literature of this country. We have created the best of its political intelligence. Yet I do not altogether regret what has happened. I shall be able to find out, if not I, my children will be able to find out whether we have lost our stamina or not. You have defined our position and have given us a popular following. If we have not lost our stamina then your victory will be brief, and your defeat final, and when it comes this nation may be transformed.'

Colonel MOORE: 'The Senator says now the seventeenth century. In the next one hundred years, from 1600 to 1700, there were only five cases of divorce.... It was a distinctively aggressive Protestant Parliament. He quotes the poet, Milton, as an authority. I do not know whether the poet Milton ever wrote on divorce.'

Dr. YEATS: 'One of the most famous of all the prose works of Milton is on divorce, which the Senator should have been taught at school.'

Colonel MOORE: 'Young people now get married knowing quite well the marriage will only last a year.'

Dr. YEATS: 'An ancient Irish form of marriage.'

Colonel MOORE: 'What is the result? If two people want a divorce, what do they do? .... These letters are written by lawyers, merely as a matter of form. Why not adopt the American method and say: "I will give a divorce to any two people who come before me. Let anybody who wants divorce have it."'

Dr. YEATS: 'I find, with regret, that I have, apparently, used the word "pressure," and am understood to mean that pressure was brought to bear on individual members. "Pressure" was not the word I wished to use, and it was not the word I had in my manuscript. It was hastily spoken. What I had in my mind was the effect of the Press, the effect of sermons, and the effect of all the letters that have been written on the feeling in this country, perfectly legitimate pressure. I had to give my speech what members thought was a religious turn, because it seemed to me that the only argument that I had to meet was a purely religious argument. I have seen no discussion in the Press and heard no discussion in this country which was not a purely religious argument, and it would be pure hypocrisy to deal with it on other grounds.'

Dr. YEATS: 'I can only speak on Senator Douglas's motion by addressing myself to the general question and I have no right to speak on the general question a second time. By way of explanation, however, I may say that I did not intend my speech to be an attack on the three great men whose statues are in our principal thoroughfares. It is probably the innate immorality of my mind that was at fault. I do not think that the memories of these great men of genius were swept away by their sexual immoralities. I still regard them as men of genius who conferred great gifts on their country. They do not cease to be men of genius because of these irregularities. To explain the extreme immorality of my mind a little further, I do not think there is any statesman in Europe who would not have gladly accepted the immorality of the renaissance if he could be assured of his country possessing the genius of the renaissance. Genius has its virtue, and it is only a small blot on its escutcheon if it is sexually irregular.'

17th December, 1925. Civil Service Regulation Bill 1925.

Dr. YEATS: 'I think perhaps it would assist us if the Minister, before the discussion goes any further, would tell us if there is any objection to scheduling the posts for which women are not eligible to stand. I think it is essential that a Government in the position of our Government should not only be in the right, but should be obviously in the right, particularly as we are after a very anarchic period, and as we have an old legacy of suspicion. The Minister said one of the objections to appointing women to certain posts is that they may get married. I wonder if that is so? My only experience of the matter has been gained in the theatre, and I have not noticed that when an actress gets married she retires from the stage. No doubt the Minister may in many cases be right, but there is the danger of making it difficult for women to marry and discouraging marriage if there is any undue discrimination against women on the ground that they will withdraw from the Service on marriage.

As I have been listening to the Minister, I have been reminded of an essay which I read in my youth by Huxley. I think he called it "Black and White." In that essay he pointed out that women did possess certain physical disabilities. They were liable to be withdrawn from service owing to certain things—child-bearing, and so on. He made one point, that it was essential that no Government should, in any way by its laws, increase these disabilities. That should be left to the process of nature. I have great confusion of mind over this Bill, because, like other Senators, I have been so absorbed in the very exciting matters which came before the Seanad in the last few days that I confess this finds some of us in a very ignorant condition, which may compel some Senators to vote against the Bill who, with greater knowledge, might vote for it. I would like that the Minister would give us all information possible on this Bill.'

3rd March, 1926. Coinage Bill 1926 Second Stage.

Mr. YEATS: 'I wish to take this opportunity to thank the Minister for Finance for the speech which he made in the Dáil promising to get together a competent, artistic committee to advise on the designs of our coinage. The official designs of the Government, especially its designs in connection with postage stamps and coinage, may be described, I think, as the silent ambassadors of national taste. The Government has now taken the right step. They may not get a beautiful coinage; it is difficult to get beauty of any kind. At any rate, the Government has the right ambition. Two days ago I had a letter from an exceedingly famous decorative artist, in which he described the postage stamps of this country as at once the humblest and ugliest in the world. At any rate, our coinage design will, I hope, be such that even the humblest citizen will be proud of it.'

24th March 1926. School Attendance Bill Second Stage 1926.

Dr. YEATS: 'I had hoped that Senator Brown would be here and that it would not have fallen on me to speak on this measure. Since this Bill passed through the Dáil much new evidence has come to our hands, which, I think, we should take into consideration. I have been reading the reports of the various inspectors. I think I will have the feeling of the Seanad with me when I say that we should not force the children into schools unless we have such assurance from the Government as will make us satisfied that these schools will be put into a fit condition to receive the children. I will read here the words of one of the inspectors: "There is a very considerable number of school buildings ill-adapted in the first case to serve as schools, and now in a bad state of repair, damp, uncomfortable, and often insanitary. A few are mere hovels, yet frequently overcrowded, a menace to the health of the children and teachers, an eyesore to the passers-by and a standing reflection on all responsible for their condition." That is an extract from the report by Mr. Tierney. He has reported on the general condition of the schools in his area. He is inspector for Mayo, part of Leinster, the whole of County Longford, and portions of Westmeath. You have practically in every inspector's report something of the same kind. A majority of the schools are not in this condition but evidently a very considerable minority of the schools are in this condition.

Speaking on this matter on the 11th June last the President said:

Before I leave this question of primary education, I should mention that there is one further matter— also an important matter in our quest for efficiency—with which the Minister for Education hopes to deal as soon as possible. This country has always suffered from the inadequacy of its school buildings. The disturbances of recent years have left us still more seriously in arrears in this important particular, and the operation of an effective School Attendance Act will increase still more the lack of proper accommodation for primary education. To meet this difficulty the Department of Education is having a thorough census made of the primary school-buildings of the Saorstát, and when this is complete, it may be necessary to ask you to make further provision in the Estimates to bring the primary school accommodation up to the level necessary for complete efficiency.

Now we have not had those further statistics as to the state of the schools. We do not know whether the Government will be able, whether it will get that necessary support to put all these schools right. But it should be our business to see that it gets that support. I should like also to suggest to the Seanad that the proper method of doing this is not under the Estimates. I hold that this should be done by a national loan. It is a non-recurrent expenditure, precisely the kind of expenditure that is usually met by a loan. One feels that if the vote is put on the Estimates that it will not be adequately and amply dealt with. I would like to do something further. I suggest to the Government that they should appoint a commission to consider the whole question of school buildings in the State. A great effort should be made to put these schools right, and that means that the attention of the country should be drawn to the matter. Furthermore, we should see that the right methods are taken and that the right form of school buildings is adopted. The Government has already a commission inquiring into the school curriculum, but they have not a commission set up for the purpose of inquiring into the school buildings. My suggestion is that it should be a point of honour to the Seanad not to ask the school children to enter those buildings until they are certain that these buildings are fit to receive the children.

To be able to do my duty as a Senator in relation to this question, I, myself, before this Government report was put into my hands, saw a number of the schools. I saw schools in Dublin and in the country. I was shocked by what I saw in the Dublin schools. I saw schools where the children were learning their lessons by artificial light at noon-day, because the windows were too small. I saw schools where two classes were being held side by side, because there was not room to give a separate class to each. That means wear and tear to the nerves of the children and to the temper of the teachers.

I also saw another thing to which I wish to draw the attention of the Government. Many of these schools are filthy. A minority of the children who come to them, I should say a substantial minority, are filthy. There are no adequate basins, sometimes no basins at all, in which the children could wash themselves. I have seen schools where the children are perfectly clean. I have seen one school in Dublin where the floors are washed once a week and brushed every day. Many of the country schools are never washed at all. I have seen a school lately in a South of Ireland town managed by the Sisters of Mercy, and it is a model to all schools. There the part of the house that is used frequently is washed once a week and brushed daily. The children are perfectly clean. What can be done there can be done elsewhere in Ireland. But you cannot have these things done unless the country is prepared to spend the money.

It should be a matter of honour to the State no matter how poor it may be, to spend that money. You must not, for instance, do what is almost always done—get this work done by the children. It must not be the business of the children to keep the school clean after they have done their day's work in the school. There must be properly appointed people to see that the school is clean and also to see that the children are clean and that they are sent to school clean. When the children are not clean they should be made wash themselves in a proper place provided in the school. If you do not do that you will not have a centre of civilisation in the schools and the children might as well remain at home. I think you cannot secure any of these things without more expense, and, of course, a more efficient system of inspection, than you have at present. The inspectors who come from the central authority will not be able to keep an eye on all these things. There is an obvious way out of the difficulty, a way which we cannot take, perhaps, but a way which the North of Ireland has taken, and that is to put the care of the school buildings in the hands of local committees.

One of the Government inspectors strongly urges that upon the Government. That is done practically all over Europe. It is done in Catholic Austria as it is done in Protestant Scandinavia. The committees differ from country to country. They are constituted in various ways, but I think these committees exist practically everywhere. I should like to add that the difficulty in appointing those committees does not come from one religion alone. It comes just as much, if I understand it, from the religion in which I was born as it comes from any other, but it is not to the credit of the State that no way can be found out of the difficulty. If we cannot have local inspection, which would mean inspection by inspectors who have local knowledge, then we must devise some equally efficient method.

There is one thing on which I feel strongly. As long as you carry on the present obsolete method of education in your schools you will have the usual strain between the master and the pupil. You will have the usual problem of children being punished by a master with a bad temper, and your only way to prevent that is when the so-called punishment books are regularly kept. Those are books in which the teacher is bound to record the punishment inflicted, and why it is inflicted. My experience is that those punishment books are not kept because there is not sufficiently adequate inspection. I do not say that the present inspectors are not most able men, but you want more numerous inspection or better local inspection to secure efficiency in those things. If the Government can convince me that it is able and willing to make these buildings suitable for the children, that is to say, to make them clean and sanitary—and many of them are not sanitary—to make the floor space sufficient and to make them reasonably cheerful, I am prepared to give my unimportant vote in favour of this Bill. If they do not, I cannot give it.

I am not asking anything extravagant. I think we ought to do whatever is done by other countries of the same wealth as this nation in order to ensure the welfare of our children. We should consider, for instance, that there are at present some arrangements, not I think always very wise, as to the feeding of school-children in the towns. There are none in the country, and judging by my own countryside, where I live during the summer months, it is needed. Children will start early in the morning. They will be the greater portion of the day in school and they will have no adequate meals. They come away hungry, and it seems, if not very necessary, at least very desirable that they should have food. Then, of course, many other countries, perhaps not richer than this, have found means of seeing that children are properly clothed and that they have proper books. These are all difficult but desirable things.

I have no desire to speak on the question of the curriculum. It is being considered by a Commission at this moment. I wish that the Government had introduced a comprehensive educational measure dealing with all the details before asking us to compel children, by law, to go into the schools. Whether it is good for the children or not depends not only on the building but on the nature of the system under which they are taught. I am sure for a child to spend all day in school with a stupid, ill-trained man under an ill-planned system, is less good for that child than that the child should be running through the fields and learning nothing. I should like to draw the attention of the Government to one nation which has reformed its educational system in the most suggestive and profound way; that is Italy. It has not produced a system unique to Italy. It has simply gathered together the results of experiments all over the world. They are now teaching a system of education adapted to an agricultural nation like this or Italy, a system of education that will not turn out clerks only, but will turn out efficient men and women who can manage to do all the work of the nation. This system has been tried in Ireland. There are some schools carrying it out. There is one large primary school managed by nuns in the South of Ireland which has adopted practically the entire Italian system and which is carrying it out with great effect, and has found that it is applicable, and that its teachers do not need special training to carry it out. The Italian Minister who adopted that policy was warned by everyone that it would not be possible to get this elaborate system carried out by partly educated people. It has been proved possible and of great benefit to the children.

In order to give an intelligent vote —at one time I thought it would be a silent one—on this question I have kept two clear principles in my mind. One is that we ought to be able to give the child of the poor as good an education as we give to the child of the rich. Of course the rich man's child remains longer at school. I have consulted teachers and people accustomed to the latest methods of education, and they are all clear that there is no reason why the education of the children of the poor should not be as good, while it lasts, as the education of the children of the rich. I would like to suggest another principle, that the child itself must be the end in education. It is a curious thing how many times the education of Europe has drifted into error. For two or three centuries people thought that their various religious systems were more important than the child. In the modern world the tendency is to think of the nation; that it is more important than the child. In Japan, I understand, the child is sacrificed to patriotism. I have seen education unified in America, so that the child is sacrificed to that of unified Americanism, and the human mind is codified. We are bound to go through the same passion ourselves. There is a tendency to subordinate the child to the idea of the nation. I suggest that whether we teach either Irish history, Anglo-Irish literature or Gaelic, we should always see that the child is the object and not any of our special purposes.'

30th March, 1926. Central Fund Bill, Second Stage, 1926.

Dr. YEATS: 'I remember when I was a boy meeting an elderly man going to vote for the County Council in Acton, and I said to him: "You know nothing about County Council affairs, really?" "No," he said, "I know nothing whatever; I do not know one man there more than another, but there is one man who is going to spend money and I am going to vote for him." I said "why," and he said, "because he has everyone against him," and he added a little later, "he must be a man of conviction."

Now I rise to ask for more consideration for those men of conviction who think that the vote on the estimates for Irish education is completely inadequate. I am not sure that I should have raised the question except for the very surprising speech made by Senator Sir John Keane in the last debate, when he said that whatever was spent upon making the Irish schools sanitary for the children should be taken by economies out of the present votes for Irish schools. We have all great respect for Senator Sir John Keane as a financial expert. I can only suppose he made that statement because he had never given any attention whatever to the question. I have gone to quite obvious sources to get the latest information. I have gone to the Encyclopedia Britannica and one or two other obvious sources, and I want to draw attention to the fact that in Ireland we spend on education only £1 6s. 0d. per head of the population; in Scotland they spend about £2 10s. 0d. per head of the population. That is to say, they spend £11,000,000 as against our four-and-a-half millions, having a population about one-third greater than ours. In England they spend about £2 10s. per head of the population on education. In the North of Ireland they lately increased their parliamentary grant for education, while they have also added to it by rates, and therefore they are spending more on education than we are. It is impossible, at the moment, to find the exact figure. Let us turn now to other small countries which we are accustomed to compare with ourselves and see how they deal with education. Denmark is spending about £2 15s. 0d. per head on education. Norway is spending about the same, £2 15s. 0d. per head, on education. I do not know what endowments, apart from parliamentary expenditure, Denmark and Norway have, but I think I can safely say that England and Scotland have far greater endowments for education than this country and that there is a further increase from this source in the amount of money spent on education in England and Scotland.

President Cosgrave said on the 11th June last year he was quite aware of the fact that there would have to be an increased grant for Irish education. I am not therefore in any way criticising the Government. I am sure that they know these figures and are anxious adequately to finance Irish education, but I think it is important this House should know these figures. I do not think the President's proposed method of dealing with the question is the most desirable. He spoke of an increase in the Estimates. I think that will lead, especially at this time of depression, to the sum voted being entirely inadequate to make the schools even tolerably sanitary, and I think the right method is through a national loan. The whole sum ought not to fall upon this generation. The repayment of it should be distributed over several generations; but when you have put the schools right you require money to keep them right. Inspectors of schools have pointed out in reports that managers have no funds to keep the schools clean and in repair and some other method will have to be found obviously.

I see by the "Irish Times" this morning that the Executive of the Irish National Teachers' Association has put down a resolution for its coming conference in favour of local committees, and of a rate to keep the schools in repair, and to keep them in a sanitary condition. The "Irish Times" article draws special attention to the fact that these bodies will be representative of the parents and that it is essential to have representatives of the parents if the schools are to be kept in a condition approximating in comfort and health to the homes in which the children live. The "Irish Times" article was very vigorous and very thoughtful, and I should think it should help to remove a good deal of the opposition to the local committees that is exhibited at present by certain managers belonging to the Church of Ireland. I think the Teachers' Association will have to use their utmost vigour to rouse public opinion if the Government is to do what they consider right in this matter. It will be said: Can we afford to make the schools sanitary considering how poor we are? I can only use the words of the Australian Minister for Education when questioned in the same way; he said: "It is precisely because we are poor that we must spend money on our schools."

I doubt if any nation can become prosperous unless it has national faith, and one very important part of national faith is faith in its resources, faith both in the richness of its soil and the richness of its intellect, and I am convinced that as much wealth can come from the intellect of Ireland as will come from the soil and that the one will repay cultivation as much as the other.'

26th April, 1926. School Attendance Bill, 1925, Third Stage.

Dr. YEATS: 'I should like to draw the attention of the Seanad to Article I. of the Convention of Geneva which, I understand, was signed by the representative of the Irish Free State:

"Children under the age of fourteen years may not be employed or worked in any public or private agricultural undertaking, or any branch thereof, save outside the hours fixed for school attendance. If they are employed outside the hours of school attendance the employment shall not be such as to prejudice their attendance at school."

That Article certainly represents the opinion of the great majority of those identified with the teaching of children all over the world, and I do not think the Free State should depart from it. It is very doubtful if it is keeping within the spirit of it, as it is, in view of the exemptions that are given at certain seasons of the year, but I am quite certain the Seanad will not support any resolution which makes further breaches in the Convention of Geneva. I would like to point out to the Seanad again that we are spending on the education of our children what amounts to £1 5s. per head of the population per annum. In England and Scotland they spend about £2 10s. per head of the population per annum. Our trade rival, Denmark, spends what amounts to about £2 15s. per head of the population. In Norway the proportion is about the same. Of course that is counting not only taxes but rates, and shows that already our education is starved. It is certain that our children are going into the battle of life very poorly equipped to face rivals, to put it no higher. In any case the children are going into the battle of life unequipped because enough is not spent on education. The proposal in the amendment is that the inefficient education the children are being given should be made still more inefficient.'

15th June, 1926. Message from the Dail.

CATHAOIRLEACH: .The following Message has been received from the Dáil:—

Tá Dáil Eireann tar éis an Rún so leanas do rith, agus is mian leo aontú Sheanaid Eireann leis:—

"Go bhfuil sé oiriúnach Có-Choiste de dhá Thigh an Oireachtais có-dhéanta de thriúr ball den Dáil agus de thriúr ball den tSeanad agus comhacht acu chun fios do chur ar dhaoine, ar pháipéirí agus ar bhreacacháin, do chur ar bun chun a fhiosrú agus a thuairisciú, an mí-chumas a cuirtar ar aicmí áirithe daoine le hAltanna 51 agus 57 den Acht Timpeal Toghachán, 1923 (Uimh. 12 de 1923) agus ná leigeann go dtoghfí iad chun aon Tighe den Oireachtas ná go suidhfidís mar bhaill den Tigh sin, ar cheart an mí-chumas san do chur ar aon aicme no aicmí eile daoine agus, más ceart, cadé an aicme no cadiad na haicmí eile ar cheart an mí-chumas san do chur."

Dáil Eireann has passed the following Resolution, in which the concurrence of Seanad Eireann is desired:—

"That it is expedient that a Joint Committee of both Houses of the Oireachtas consisting of three members of the Dáil and three members of the Seanad, with power to send for persons, papers and records, be set up to inquire and report whether the incapacity to be elected to, or to sit as a member of, either House of the Oireachtas imposed as regards certain classes of persons by Sections 51 and 57 of the Electoral Act, 1923 (No. 12 of 1923) should be extended to include any other class or classes of persons, and, if so, to what class or classes should the incapacity extend."

Mr. YEATS: 'We have all great respect for President Cosgrave. He is not a member of this House but he comes to us and asks us to appoint a Committee which would possibly disqualify certain members of this House from the right to be elected to sit in the Seanad. I feel we owe it to the honour and dignity of this House not to permit any kind of committee or tribunal calling in question their right to be elected and sit here, unless a very strong case indeed can be made for it. We had a resolution brought forward at first without the intention of making any case for it whatever. We have to use a great effort to get any sort of statement of facts whatever. I do not think any member of this House understood the first statement made by the President.

It is most necessary that we should have the assistance in our Legislature of the best technical types. In the near future, we shall have to consider many things in connection with education, and it is most necessary that the opinions of the teachers should be represented in both Houses. In the recent debates in the Dáil one man whose knowledge and opinion were of the utmost value to the Dáil was a teacher —Deputy O'Connell. No member of either House, as far as I can make out by a careful study of his and other speeches, possesses knowledge comparable to his on the whole question of education in this country. I do not think that his position will be affected by this Committee, but where a man of such technical knowledge has been found once he can be found again. We require to have that technical knowledge in this House for the next two or three years. I hope I am a benevolent man, and I think I am an unsuspicious man, but I find it difficult to separate this resolution from some preceding events.

Some months ago an organisation of teachers passed a resolution in favour of local control of school buildings, that is to say, that these buildings should be controlled and kept in order by local committees.

Very considerable opposition arose to that object from the managers, and it is only right I should say not from the managers of one denomination only but a very considerable opposition came also from the Protestant managers, who did not like Protestant schools passing under the control of Catholic committees.

It is not a sectarian question. It is a question of the ecclesiastical mind, Protestant and Catholic on the one side and on the other a very great deal of the most intelligent lay opinion in Ireland. Then two or three weeks ago the Catholic Managerial Association passed a resolution in favour of repairs to schools and claiming that the money for the repairs should be given to the managers for that purpose, and they added to the resolution a rider that the schools in Ireland are in a fairly good condition, which they are not. They know the arrangements for the maintenance of schools have broken down, and it was admitted that the schools are now in a bad condition. I read in the papers that "Certain pressure was brought upon the President." I think that is the diplomatic and journalistic way of putting it, and then we have this resolution. As I have said, the President, a man for whom we have the utmost respect, has come and asked us to appoint a tribunal to consider the eligibility of certain of our members. I suggest that behind the President there is a certain pressure asking him to have a tribunal appointed. I think a much stronger case must be made before this House votes for the establishment of any such tribunal.'

14th July, 1926. The Lane Pictures.

Dr. YEATS: 'It will be within the memory of Senators that some two years ago both this House and the Dáil passed resolutions urging the British Government to give effect to the unwitnessed codicil of Sir Hugh Lane's will. Lord Glenavy gave his very emphatic opinion at the time that it was impossible to doubt that Sir Hugh Lane did intend that codicil as his last will and testament. The only satisfactory thing in the report issued some two weeks ago by the British Government is that it also decides that Sir Hugh Lane did intend that codicil for his last will and testament. Senator Brown and others have analysed and exposed the excuses made by the Commission and accepted by the British Government for not giving effect to that decision. In this country we have to decide upon a course of action, and it is largely with that object that I speak. It has been a long dispute; some of us have given much time and thought to it; my closest friend, Lady Gregory, has given the best of her thought and much of her time to it for the last ten years. The property involved, though great in monetary value, is more than property, for it means the possession of the implements of national culture. You will forgive me if I forget that I am occasionally a politician, and remember that I am always a man of letters and speak less diplomatically and with less respect for institutions and great names than is, perhaps, usual in public life. In our endeavour to have our case laid before the British public once more, to have the fallacies of this report exposed, we are faced with an unexpected difficulty. Three weeks ago, while the report was still unissued, when the British Government had announced no decision, when the whole matter was *sub-judice* between the nations, the King opened the new wing of the Tate Gallery, that is to say, the building which, it is claimed, was built to contain these pictures by Sir Joseph Duveen, and of which they are the principal ornament. As he made his speech, or as he passed through the gallery to deliver it, his eyes must constantly have looked upon the words, "Lane Bequest."

It is the policy of most of us in this country, seeing that very lately we preferred a king to a president and that we fought a civil war that we might be governed by a king rather than a president, to remain upon the friendliest terms with the King of England, who is also the King of Ireland. We have been told, I do not know whether truthfully or not, that the King is personally friendly to us, that a certain speech which influenced our affairs for good was made on his own initiative. Statements of that kind are frequently untrue; they are put out for policy, but, whether true or not, we have no desire to disturb the impression that they have left. Our relations with Ulster make this more essential. But it would be impossible to preserve this attitude towards Royalty if certain obvious conditions are ignored. When the King was urged to perform an action which seriously compromised the claim made by this nation, when he was urged to intervene in this international dispute, was it pointed out to him that he should be advised, not by his English Ministers alone, but also by the Governor-General, or otherwise by his Irish Ministers? We have no means of questioning Ministers in this House, and I would be glad, therefore, if someone in the Dáil would ask President Cosgrave if his Government was consulted before the King recently opened the new modern gallery in London. Important as our claim for the Lane pictures is, this question seems to me to raise an issue of far greater importance, one vitally affecting the constitutional position not only of this country but of every Dominion. I can imagine the British Government replying in the evasive spirit of its Commission that as our claim was moral and not legal the King was not bound to take cognizance of it, but in disputes between nations— and the British Government itself has, within its terms of reference to the Commission, called this dispute international—it is not legal but moral and material issues that cause trouble. A day may come when the action of the King may prejudice some claim involving the most fundamental rights. I see by the daily papers that Canada and the Irish Free State are to seek at the next Imperial Conference for some clarification or modification of the relations between the Crown and the Dominions. I think that this recent experience of ours shows that one or the other is necessary.

When I addressed this House some two years ago on this question I believed that our case was almost won, and from that day to about three weeks before the issue of the report we had continual assurances that it had been practically decided in our favour. The persons who gave us these assurances seemed to be in a position to know. I am certain of their sincerity. If you ask me about the sincerity of those from whom they derived their information, I can merely say that I am without conviction, one way or the other. What happened at the last moment is unknown to me. I am sure of one thing; it was not any particular force or authority in the report of the Commission that made the change. Senator Brown has dealt effectively with the two or three reasons which they give for retaining in London property which they admit that Sir Hugh Lane intended for Dublin, and believe that he had legally bequeathed to Dublin. Of these arguments, that which seems to have weighed most with English public opinion, and probably with the Commission, is the statement put forward by the Tate Gallery and accepted by the Commission, that Sir Joseph Duveen received a promise on June 9th, 1916, that if he were to build a new wing to the Tate Gallery Sir Hugh

Lane's pictures should be deposited there. I hold letters in my hand which will prove conclusively that no such promise was ever given. Those letters were not laid before the Commission, because it never passed through the minds of the three witnesses, Lady Gregory, Mrs. Shine and myself, that the Commission would go outside its reference, nor did it occur to the Commissioners to question us upon this point. They had been appointed to find out whether Sir Hugh Lane intended the codicil to be a legal document, and whether, if so, considering the international issue involved, it should be given effect to. It never occurred to us that they would repudiate their reference, and declare that there was no international issue involved, and then go into a mass of detail which seemed excluded by that reference. Before repudiating their reference they should have referred the matter back to the English Government for a new reference, and have informed us of their action. If such a promise had been given, it would have carried no weight, for it would have been given by one party in the dispute without the knowledge of the other, but it was not given, as I shall now show.

Sir Hugh Lane was drowned in the "Lusitania" on May 7th, 1915, and at the end of that month Lady Gregory laid the codicil before the Chairman of the Board of Governors of the English National Gallery, which had the custody of the pictures. I have here a letter written by her on June 6th of that year to a great New York connoisseur and collector:

"I went to see (taking a copy of the codicil) Lord Curzon, the most active of the London National Gallery trustees, and one who appreciates most the French pictures. He would, of course, like to keep them but said he thought Hugh's wishes, so clearly expressed, ought to be respected, and he would say that when the time comes to the other trustees."

On June 1st, 1915, that is to say, three or four days before the date of the letter I have just quoted, Lady Gregory received the following letter from Lord Curzon:

"I mentioned to-day to the National Gallery Board the subject which you had been good enough to bring before me the evening before ....I think the right thing would be for the executors to address them formally through solicitors, and lay the whole case before them."

On September 15th Lord Curzon wrote as follows:

"It seems to be a matter in which the executors will have to formally approach the Board, who will, no doubt, consult their solicitors."

A year later I was in London and heard privately that the National Gallery intended to have a gallery built for modern French pictures, and to put the Lane collection into it. I told Lady Gregory of this, and she wrote to Lord Curzon, who answered as follows on October 10th, 1916:

"The matter is not in my hands nor at this moment even in the hands of the Board. They are waiting to be advised by their legal advisers, and in the interim it would not be right for any individual trustee to intervene."

Yet our opponents allege, and the Commission accepts their allegation, that an individual trustee did intervene. Here are the words of the report:

"Not only has the London Gallery the legal possession of the pictures but, on the assurance that such a gift would be in perpetuity, it has secured the gift of a gallery in which the pictures are to be housed."

An editorial in the Burlington Magazine for 1924 gives the precise date and circumstance of the alleged promise:

"On June 9th, 1916, Sir Joseph Duveen, being on the point of returning to America, saw Lord D'Abernon about the project."

It then goes on to say that Lord D'Abernon thereupon promised the pictures if Sir Joseph Duveen built the gallery.

I have read you the assurances of the Chairman of the Board, Lord Curzon, stating that the matter was undecided, assurances repeated several times for more than a year, the last and most specific, that in which he states that no individual governor had the right to intervene, being written some months after the date of the alleged promise. Relying upon those repeated assurances we had summoned no meetings, organised neither petitions nor protest, and we were right. It was entirely impossible that a man of Lord Curzon's position and training would have deliberately deceived us. Unless minutes of the National Gallery recording that promise were laid before the Commission, I have a right to affirm that such a promise was never given. Sir Joseph Duveen or Mr. McCall imagined the whole thing, or Lord D'Abernon made some vague statement which was misinterpreted. The matter is very serious, a very large amount of property is involved, property which may already be worth some £200,000 and which will certainly rise in value from year to year. I, therefore, ask the Irish Government to press upon the British Government the production of the minutes of the Board of Governors of the National Gallery of London for the period during which the promise is stated to have been made. If no such minute can be discovered then the Commission has been grossly misled; if it is discovered, we have.

I was going to deal with the other indefinite argument, that if Sir Hugh Lane had lived he would have changed his mind. He was the most generous of men. A famous artist said of him that he had raised the profession of a picture dealer into the magnificence of the Medici. Had he lived I have no doubt he would have given great endowments right and left to Dublin, to London, and to that great gallery in South Africa that was partly his foundation. But when he was going on that last voyage he knew he had only one collection of pictures to bequeath. He preferred to bequeath them, where the rest of his bequests had gone, to the gallery which will always bear his name, where everything had been chosen by himself, and where they were not to be lost among the growing richness of the great London gallery.

There is that other argument—I am not competent to deal with it—that there is no precedent for altering a will. While we do not press that point I have heard great lawyers differ on it. The other day the "Independent" newspaper—and I should like to thank the "Independent" newspaper for the great vigour with which it is pressing this question—gave a very remarkable precedent. In the midst of the Great War, by Act of Parliament, the will of Cecil Rhodes was modified. In that case there was no question of the letter of the will or of his intentions. He had left a large bequest to enable German students to attend certain English universities. They abrogated that request not merely for the time of the war but for ever. That is precisely one of those actions which all nations do in time of war and are ashamed of afterwards. Yet it seems to me if we had claimed that we would not make an excessive claim. It seems to me what they did by Act of Parliament to modify the will of Cecil Rhodes under the influence of national hatred they might well be asked to do—to modify the will of Sir Hugh Lane under the influence of national honour. Now what are we to do? No compromise. We ask and we must continue to ask our right—to hold 39 pictures, and for ever. Let the Dublin Commissioners build that long-promised gallery. We have already, in Harcourt Street, great treasures that will make it one of the richest galleries in the world. Let them build that gallery and let them see there is ample space for those 39 pictures. Let them write the names of the pictures on the wall, in spaces reserved for them, and let the codicil be displayed in some conspicuous place and watch the public opinion of these countries. I do not believe that the public opinion of these countries will permit the London Gallery to retain pictures which it was not the intention of the donor to leave to it.'

22nd July, 1926. High Court and Supreme Court Rules

Dr. YEATS: 'I move:—

"To insert before the word "received" the word "not" and to add at the end of the motion the words "with the exception of Order 30, Rules 2 and 3."

This amendment is to delete that portion of the rules which prescribes the present robes and wigs of the Judges of the High Court and the Supreme Court. I move this, not because I desire to see the judges sitting in their courts in ordinary costume, but because I believe that the Government have in their possession very much finer designs than any that has come down to us. I am sorry that the Government have not found some means of making these designs known to this House, because the House has to vote on the subject. They might have been laid on the Table of the House. You are asked to vote in favour of designs without knowing what the alternative to these designs is. The only guidance that this House might perhaps possess is that new designs have been adopted for the District Court, and photographs of these designs have appeared in the papers.'

Dr. YEATS: 'They have not adopted any costumes, but we have seen the costumes that have been reproduced. They are certainly very dignified and very simple. They are, I think, more dignified and more simple than any costumes worn in any magistrates' courts in these islands. The robes were designed by a celebrated Irish artist, Sir Charles Shannon, and the cap was designed at the Dun Emer Works, and admirably designed. However, in the circumstances I cannot ask you to vote in favour of other designs, because I cannot put the designs before you. But I suggest if you reject the present robes and wigs, the Government will have to lay before you new designs by somebody, and then we will know whether or not we will have a better type. When you think over the present costume, that great grey wig and that gown, if you try to see it without historical associations, is it not something incredibly fantastic? Is it not something essentially preposterous? Of course, I admit that historical associations and tradition can endear anything; I will admit that the judge's wig is endeared to me by historic associations and tradition. Historical traditions have endeared the small foot of the Chinese woman, have endeared the nose-ring. I admit that I find it very difficult to realise how preposterous the judge's wig is. I am in the position of some man in China who finds it impossible to realise the preposterousness of the small foot, but it is so. Historical associations are great things. I do not think we should lightly put them aside, even when we endear something which is, in itself, without dignity or honour. Historical associations give honour and they give dignity.

But this country has passed through one of those crises which all countries have made the occasion of a new act of energy for the creation of tradition. No country that I know, after a revolution such as we have gone through, has been content to take without examination the traditions of the past, and I cannot imagine any place where innovation is more necessary than in the outward image of the law. One of the greatest arguments with which we have been familiar for generations in favour of the self-government of this country, was that the law as practised here was regarded by great numbers of people as something inherently alien. We all want the people to realise that the law is now their own creation, their own instrument, and any external change which marks that fact will in some degree—I will not say in a great degree—help the people to understand that the judges are their own judges and not judges imposed upon them from without. I speak especially of the judges. I think the case of the barristers is somewhat different. They are not paid out of public money. They are a free corporation. I should be prepared to leave the barristers to time and to public opinion. But the Government cannot put aside responsibility for the judges, because the judges are paid with Government money, and—always provided, remember, that they possess better designs, designs inherently of greater dignity and of greater nobility than those in present use—I can see every reason for the adoption of these designs, and I can see no sufficient case against the adoption. The designs for the Supreme Court and for the High Court which the Government possess are, in my belief, designs of great dignity, great beauty and simplicity. They would do honour to any country, and in adopting them this country would do as well as the Vatican did when it permitted Michael Angelo to set aside one does not know what historical traditions, and to design the costumes of the Papal Guards.'

Sir JOHN KEANE: 'Yes, English tradition. I am not ashamed to say English tradition. It is the tradition which the people have grown accustomed to. I notice that we naturally gravitate towards tradition. Let us look at all the observances and all the procedure of the two Houses of the Oireachtas. Except with the occasional appearance of the Irish language on special occasions and in official records, I venture to say our procedure is being moulded, not unnaturally, but perhaps unconsciously, on the traditions of the British Parliament.. ... I do not see why we should do violence to tradition in respect to the costume of our judges. The Senator referred to the present head-dress of our judges as preposterous, but I can conceive great practical value in that head-dress. I was looking up literary references as to what I believe is the proposed new head-dress known as the biretta. I have not much knowledge of the biretta, but I find a reference to it in the Athenæum in these words: "a person described as with a black shock of hair emerging or appearing under his red biretta." I can conceive nothing more inartistic than that, because hair may not be always black, it may be sometimes grey or brown, it may be long or short, or a person may have no hair. Moreover, we may now have ladies joining the legal profession. I see nothing in the ordinary course of development to prevent ladies rising to seats upon the Bench. Ladies have a great variety of head-dress which would also contrast in a very incongruous manner with such a close-fitting ornament as the biretta.

The wig has the virtue of uniformity and covers up all these imperfections of the flesh and gives very dignified results. You get uniformity. That is for what it is worth..... My memory at once went back to a recent speech delivered by Senator Yeats in this House on the subject of the Lane pictures, when he used these words: "You will forgive me if I forget that I am occasionally a politician and remember that I am always a man of letters, and speak less diplomatically and with less respect for institutions and great names than is, perhaps, usual in public life." Following up that trend of thought I remember certain verses of the Senator's in which his words seem to me rather inconsistent with the remarks that I have just quoted. He writes:

"All things can tempt me from this craft of verse;

One time it was a woman's face, or worse—

The seeming needs of my fool-driven land.'"

(The Green Helmet 1910)

Sir John KEANE: 'That will bring close together the outward association between the Church and the Judiciary which had been widening steadily down the ages. We find full justification in verses written by the Senator himself:

"How but in custom and in ceremony

Are innocence and beauty born?

Ceremony's a name for the rich horn

And Custom for the spreading laurel tree."'

(A Prayer for My Daughter, 1921)

If I understand that rightly, the rich horn is that of plenty which we all desire, and the laurel tree is that of fame to which we aspire.'

Dr. YEATS: 'If we assume for a moment that this is a desirable thing, that it is possible to put the judges into costumes that are appropriate to the country, do you think that a very old man, grown old in the use of quite a different costume, would ever accept the change? Never, impossible. If the change is desirable— there is no way out of it—the change would have to be imposed on the judges. If I were an old judge, who wore a wig and gown all my life, I should hate to change it. I should be furious if any man proposed it, although it might be most desirable to make a change. It is not an unimportant thing we are discussing. If we were discussing here to-day whether the Supreme Court should meet in a very imposing building, or in a building which seemed to be unworthy of the nation, we would not think it unimportant to debate the question. I suggest to you that the question of the costume in which the judge gives his decision is of greater importance than the building in which he gives it. Are we to allow very old men, for whom we have the greatest respect, to settle the tradition of this country for centuries, because it will be for centuries if now at a time of revolution when we have a chance, we do not create a tradition. Now is our opportunity.

I thank Senator Sir John Keane for his appropriate and friendly quotations from myself. I would like to say that when I talked of this "fool-driven land"—a good many years ago now— I meant that it was fool-driven in certain matters—poetry and the theatre— matters in which I felt I had a greater right to an opinion than I have in politics. Senator Sir John Keane described how a certain judge's cap—a biretta he called it—looked very inappropriate, if worn by a red-haired or a brown-haired man. I would suggest to him that when you see red or brown hair coming from under a grey wig it looks still more inappropriate.'

Amendment put. The Seanad divided: Tá, 12; Níl, 13.

24th February, 1927. Industrial and Commercial Property (Protection) Bill 1926.

Dr. YEATS: 'There has been considerable anxiety amongst Irish artists, dramatists and designers, as to how their interests will be affected by this Bill. I think it is right that I should say that I have gone into all the sections which affect their interests, and I think it is a thoroughly good Bill. I think it gives better protection to the Irish designer and dramatist—especially the dramatist—than is given by contemporary English legislation. I had a certain amount of anxiety about one or two details in the Bill as it passed the Dáil, but my anxiety has been removed by Senator Brown's speech. There was one matter on which he did not touch—that is, that the Registrar of Copyrights at Washington has refused to register the copyright of Irish authors. This has caused considerable loss.

I know one Irish author who, acting on legal advice, has published nothing for many months and thereby has suffered considerable financial loss. If you publish in England or Ireland, publication in America has to be practically simultaneous, and if you cannot register your American copyright you may, for the time being, lose it. I know the Government understands this and I know they will make their utmost endeavour, not only to restore our right of registration in the Washington Register, but to make it retrospective so that Irish books published during the interregnum will have registration given them in America. That has been my chief anxiety in connection with this Bill recently, and I know the Government is, as I say, as anxious as I am to put this matter right. I merely speak to urge them to do so quickly, because serious loss is being suffered by Irish authors.'

9th March, 1927. Merrion Square, (Dublin) Bill, 1927.

Mr. BENNETT: 'I beg to move the Second Reading of the Merrion Square (Dublin) Bill, 1927, the Title of which is as follows:—

"A Bill entitled an Act to enable the Commissioners of Merrion Square to convey and transfer to the Trustees of the Irish National War Memorial Trust the ground within Merrion Square in the City of Dublin and other property vested in the said Commissioners as such; and to provide for the transfer of the said ground to the Right Honourable the Lord Mayor, Aldermen and Burgesses of Dublin from the said Trustees when the same has been laid out as a public park; and for other purposes connected therewith."'

Dr. YEATS: 'I do not like to speak in this House unless on things I have studied—letters and art. On this occasion, however, I have no choice. I am a resident in Merrion Square. I attended the largely-attended meeting of the residents of Merrion Square to empower the Commissioners to negotiate over this matter. I have no memory for the details or the numbers at that meeting. I do not know how many people were there. I cannot even tell you the date of the meeting. But there were large numbers of residents of the Square at that meeting. I understood, too, that the larger number of those present signed the document necessary. Those of us who are in favour of the opening of the Square to the public— having the Square opened by this memorial scheme—have, I think, certain very strong arguments in our minds. We are all familiar with the argument that there might be a demonstration. We do not believe it, but if we did believe it, it would not influence us. We were not so selfish as to allow our own interests for a few years to interfere with what we believe to be the welfare of the children of Dublin for all time to come.

Very occasionally, perhaps once a year, I go and walk in that Square. We use it very little, and I notice that there are generally children there who have no legal right to be there. The railing is in bad repair and they go in. I should like those children to have a legal right to play in that Square. I should like the Square to be made available for them. Almost every day I go round the waters in Stephen's Green. I know the great delight that that Square and these waters give children. It must enter into their life and memory for ever, and just as I do not think one ought to allow our temporary but possible discomfort for a few years to interfere with the opening of this Square, I do not think we should take too seriously the interests, the fancies or desires of even those admirable men who want a great demonstration upon Armistice Day. Armistice Day will recede.

These men will not live for ever. I hope it is not going to become a permanent political demonstration in this country, to be carried on by the children of ex-Servicemen. It will grow less and less every year.

Then you have this question of the monument. I am not greatly interested in the question of the monument one way or the other but I should be very glad indeed if a dignified monument is put up in the Square or wherever the Committee decide, with the names of the men who served in the Great War. That seems to be an entirely worthy and noble ambition. Their great great grandchildren, perhaps a century hence, will go into the Square and point out the names of their ancestors upon that monument. That is a different thing from the annual demonstration of thousands in the midst of the city. I was very much surprised by something in Senator Sir Bryan Mahon's speech. He said that no matter what these ex-Servicemen were told to do they would if they preferred it, go and demonstrate in the middle of Merrion Square. Now 100,000 men do not go and demonstrate anywhere without being organised. He meant that there are ex-Servicemen who are prepared to demonstrate against the orders of their own leaders because I refuse to believe that Senator Sir Bryan Mahon and Senator Sir William Hickie would order them to demonstrate against the direction of the city and of the Government in the midst of Merrion Square. No, they would rather order them to go to the replica of the Cenotaph, an exact replica of the one in Whitehall, which I understand the promoters of this measure are quite prepared to erect in the Phoenix Park. They would, as loyal citizens, not annoy the citizens in this way, but Senator Sir Bryan Mahon thinks that there are men who will organise against that, against their own leaders and the State, will hold their own memorial service and trample down the flowers in the midst of the Square. I am sorry to say that I cannot believe Senator Sir Byran Mahon. I think he is misrepresenting the ex-Servicemen. I do not think there are such men amongst them. I think he himself has been carried away by the propaganda against this memorial. I have heard no argument against it from any resident of Merrion Square except, precisely, this argument that men would demonstrate in the Square and destroy the place, make a noise, annoy the inhabitants of the Square and make them uncomfortable. I support the scheme very heartily because I do not believe that in 100 years any monument erected now will be very important. Wellington Monument is not in a sense a very important monument. But I believe in 100 years the Square will be there if this scheme is carried out for the health of the Dublin children and the delight of all the citizens.'

11th March, 1927. Industrial and Commercial Property Protection Bill, 1926, Third Stage.

Mr. BROWN: 'I beg to move amendment 24:—

Sub-section (6), after the word "Dominions," in line 37, to insert the words "protectorate or territory."

Amendment agreed to.

Section 152, as amended, agreed to.

Section 153 agreed to.

SECTION 154.

(1) Subject to the provisions of this Act, copyright shall subsist in Saorstát Eireann for the term hereinafter mentioned in every original literary, dramatic, musical, and artistic work, if —

(a) in the case of a published worw, the work was first published within Saorstát Eireann or a part of the British dominions to which the benefit of this Part of this Act extends; and

(2) . . . .

(a) to produce, reproduce, perform, or publish any translation of the work;'

Mr. CUMMINS: 'The object of the amendment primarily is to make Dublin what it once was — a great centre of printing, one of the leading centres, perhaps, in the British Isles, when it turned out a quality of work equal to any of its kind.... I saw within the last few days in this House an example of art printing done in Dublin, and I was assured that that specimen was as excellently and as cheaply done, and, in fact, more cheaply than any similar kind of work could be done, in any part of the British Isles. I was told, further, that work which here cost 10/6 would, probably, not be turned out in the present state of English printing for less than one guinea. That is one of the objects of the amendment — to promote and encourage the printing trade in Dublin.'

Dr. YEATS: 'I think I may, perhaps, allay some of the feelings of the Senators by demonstrating, as I shall, that the proposal of Senator

Cummins is entirely absurd and unworkable. Last Monday evening a very distinguished scholar came to see me. He has devoted his life to editing texts in Middle and Old Irish. He told me that scholars and members of learned socities were alarmed. He began by pointing out to me that much has been done lately in phonetics in the vernacular, that is to say, taking down Irish dialects. It is very important work, and is an attempt to record the pronunciation of the various dialects of Ireland. They are not taken down in any alphabet of any country, but in a special set of symbols. No Irish publisher possesses those symbols. The result is that those books, recording the Irish dialect, are printed in Copenhagen and Germany. He pointed out to me that if this were passed certain scholars who have done this work, who are not citizens of the Saorstát, would possess the copyright of their work. Those who are citizens of the Saorstát would possess it in every country except their own. He then went on to point out to me that practically all works of learning are produced by certain Presses which are subvented from universities.

There is no publisher in Ireland who will accept or could accept such books. These books are brought to the University Press in Cambridge or the Clarendon Press in Oxford, or rather to the publishing houses which take their name from these Presses. Those books pay the authors practically nothing at all. The learned man is satisfied merely that his scholarship should be given to the world. If you pass this law these men will have copyright in every country except their own. I should add further that in publishing a work of this kind it is not only necessary to find the publisher who will take your work and pay for the printing, but it is desirable to find the publisher who has that very expensive thing — a highly-paid trained "reader to the press." No Irish publisher possesses it, as I know to my cost, but it is of enormous importance when dealing with works of learning. It may be said that as these learned men cannot be published except by subventioned presses, no matter what law you pass, they will not be printed in Ireland; that they should be left out of the argument.

We are thinking of the future. This is an ill-educated country. We all hope that will change. You are dealing with works 50 years after the death of the author. Such copyright may be all he has to leave to his children; some of these books, years and years hence, may be of considerable value. There are other works of scholarship which are of immediate value. At the Cambridge University Press are published great universal histories. One, a modern history, is finished. The Ancient History and Medieval History are unfinished. These are the works of a great many different scholars. One scholar's work may run into 300 pages. The work of these texts is done by University scholars. Those are men who cannot change their citizenship. Those men who have done this work cannot set up British citizenship. At once on the publication of this great universal history an Irish publisher can take 300 pages out, perhaps, the research of a man's life, and publish it here. Probably when this many volumed ancient history is completed it may contain a large section on Early Ireland, hundreds of pages that could be taken out immediately and published in this country.

It is quite obvious that no Irish author, no matter how patriotic, could persuade publishers of these universal histories to print in Ireland. They are always printed in certain University Presses which have a subvention from the university. I will give you another example. Many Irish scholars have done work on the Encyclopedia Britannica. They cannot very well persuade publishers of the Encyclopedia Britannica to print in Ireland.'

Mrs. WYSE POWER: 'They are not publishers….only employed to do the work.'

Dr. YEATS: 'I do not understand the point of that. The editors of the Encyclopedia will get their lives of O'Connell, of Burke, and of Parnell from Irish writers. Those authors will not succeed in inducing the great Encyclopedia Britannica Company to change their whole habits of printing and print in Ireland. The idea is absurd. The Irish publisher can extract these lives of O'Connell, Burke and Parnell, containing the latest information on their subjects, and can publish them here, and what is more there is at present no law whatever which can prevent him sending them to England. Anyone can write from England, as they write at present to an Irish bookseller, and ask for such a book. At present there is no machinery to stop these books from going into England. What will happen is, Irish scholars will not be employed because they have only an impaired copyright to offer. I am sure no one in this House wishes to do this great injury to Irish scholars. That, I think, we are agreed to.

I dare say, however, when they come to considering a creative writer they are in a different sphere. There is the idea that a creative writer is making a great deal of money. They have in their imagination that he is. A few are singularly wealthy men—Mr. George Bernard Shaw, Mr. Arnold Bennett, and Mr. H.G. Wells. These men are exceptional. No doubt they can dictate to their publishers and tell them where they are to print. If the publisher does not agree to print wherever they dictate they can say: "I will go to another publisher." Remember an old couplet of the eighteenth century. It is not far out when you go over in your own mind the lives of men whose work has become immortal. It is:

"Seven Grecian cities fought for Homer dead,

Through which the living Homer begged his bread."

Very few authors win success before they reach 40 years of age. Very few authors, no matter what their later careers, are in a position to change their publishers or dictate to their publishers. One young Irish novelist of to-day has, I know, made an agreement for a term of years. His publisher pays him so much a year and he gives him all he produces. That man loses his copyright unless he declares himself a British citizen. You are compelling export of your authors. Perhaps I might be a little personal. At the start I wish to say that I have had a very smooth and easy career. I make no complaint whatever. I was 45 before I ever earned from my books or by serial publication of their contents, as much as the £4 a week earned by Irish printers. During the last four or five years of that time I was able to enlarge my income by lecturing. I was not in a position to change my publisher. My publisher was Mr. A.H. Bullen. He had a rather famous Press — the Shakespeare Head Press. I cannot see myself going to Mr. A.H. Bullen, who had given me beautifully printed books, and who took me at a time another publisher refused me, and saying: "I shall withdraw unless you change your printers." Even much more celebrated men than I am have had the same experience even towards the end of their lives. Robert Browning told Lady Gregory that he would have made more money at any profession, even making matches. He was not in a position to change his publisher. Do you think it is a dignified position for a nation to say: "You will not have copyright in Ireland unless you can cajole your publisher; speak smooth to him"? Cajole! that is what you want authors to do. You are passing a law of cajolery.

I notice another result to which I wish to draw your attention. No Irish author can serialise his work in the English Press or newspapers and keep his copyright. No author, I think, however successful, who is dependent on his work for a living can afford to give up serialising his work in the English Press. Just as you have no Irish publishers prepared to take Irish authors' work, you have no Irish magazines or Irish newspapers prepared at their own expense to undertake the serialising of authors' work, and give anything like adequate pay for it; if they could pay for it at all. One Irish author — I will not mention names — a very celebrated woman, has at this moment ready for publication an autobiography covering many years and dealing with many things and personalities important in Irish history. It deals also with many great English, social and political questions. That autobiography will be serialised in the English Press. If this law is passed it will be immediately pirated by the Irish Press, which will not pay a penny to the author. It will also be pirated in book form. You cannot compel an English newspaper or review to print in Ireland for the sake of one contribution. It would be preposterous. So far as the copyright of books is concerned I do not suppose it personally will affect me. I have done the bulk of my work. Can I go to my publisher and say: "I want you to print in Ireland?" If he says "No," what am I to do? He has all my works, my collected edition: I lose heavily if I detach my work from that uniform edition, and have broken faith with those who purchased that edition on the understanding that it is to be a genuine collected edition. Cajolery! This great State is going to pass a law by which people are to be cajoled to do what it wants. I will not leave this country because you appropriate my books, the few I have to write. If you made it impossible for me or any Irish author to serialise our work our incomes would suffer. I shall not leave this country, but shall move to the border, and I assure you I shall become exceedingly eloquent if I do.

There is no reason in the world why this town should not become a centre of printing and publishing. I am not speaking in entire ignorance. I have some little experience. Some 25 years ago at the establishment of the Abbey Theatre I became editor of the Cuala Press. It is a hand press which employs several Irish printers all the year round. Nearly all my first editions have been printed by that Press. The first editions of a great many writers were printed there. As it is now the longest established hand press in these islands I have a right to say we have succeeded. There is no reason why what we have done in a small way cannot be done by this country on a large scale. If you are to do it on a large scale you must do the work as well and as cheaply as it is done elsewhere. There is a misunderstanding about printing. The artisan prints well. He seldom does bad work. The bad work that prevents your publishers and printers succeeding is done because they have not men of taste to select type, arrange proper proportions, margins, binding and the other necessaries of well-turned-out books. You can make a great centre of publishing and printing here, because Ireland has a good literary prestige in the world now. But, if you got all the Irish authors in the world to publish here they would not be, in themselves, sufficient in number to make it a great publishing centre. If you are going to make it even a paying centre for printing and publishing, apart from making it a great centre, you must keep the goodwill of the publishers of the world, and you must keep the goodwill of the men of letters of the world. You will certainly not do so by what will be considered all over Europe as pirating. The educated opinion of Europe sees no difference between the property in a book and the property in an article of manufacture. You would not think of confiscating Jacob's biscuits because the tin in which they are put up was not made in Ireland. That is the educated opinion of Europe.

I have here a document to which I would like to draw the attention of those interested in Irish publishing. Some time ago a book by an Irish author was printed in America. I have a protest signed by 150 men, whose names are those of men of great eminence all over Europe. I will mention some of these names. They are from all countries.

Germany is represented by that man often described as the greatest mathematician and man of science of our day — Einstein. There are appended the names of other celebrated German authors. Russia is represented by the President of the famous Russian Academy of Letters. Spain is represented by the President of the Spanish Academy, Azorin; the most celebrated of her dramatists, Benavente, and the great Catholic philosopher, Miguel de Unamuno. Italy is represented by her Minister of Education, Giovanni Gentile, who is also a very great philosopher, and who it may be of interest to some Senators to know has organised the entire education of Italy in a way of far greater perfection than any educational system of Europe. It may be also well to know that he has restored religious education to the schools. Austria is represented by Hofmannsthal, a very great dramatist and poet. Belgium is represented by the dramatist, Maurice Maeterlinck, and France is represented by various members of the French Academy of great eminence. England is represented by a great many names, such as John Galsworthy and Bertram Russell.

That appeal is not merely an appeal to American opinion to condemn piracy; it is an appeal to advertisers to withdraw all advertisements from the publisher who has committed this act of piracy. Do you think Irish publishing houses will flourish if they carry on piracy of that kind? No, decidedly not. The world has become sensitive in recent years on the question of literary copyright, because it involves the prestige of men of letters in all countries. You can only make a successful publishing or printing house here if you keep the goodwill of publishers and the goodwill of men of letters.'

Colonel MOORE: 'I had every wish to vote in favour of the amendment, but I must confess that after hearing Senator Yeats I have been completely changed in my opinion....'

Amendment withdrawn.

7th April, 1927. Merrion Square (Dublin) Bill 1927.

Dr. YEATS: 'I want to ask a question of the promoters of the Bill. The wisdom of the decision of the Dáil has been very much discussed, and I think it would help the community to give an enlightened decision if my question were answered. If this Bill passed, the people of Dublin would have come into possession of Merrion Square as a park for ever. I understand that the trustees of the Pembroke Estate will in twelve years be at liberty to sell Merrion Square as a building site. It is inconceivable that the Dublin Commissioners should desire or, if they could prevent it, should permit that great open space to be built over. I have heard, however, a very high sum mentioned as the price the Commissioners will have to pay for Merrion Square if they have to buy it. There is no doubt that they would have to pay for its building value. I would be obliged if you, sir, would permit Senator Jameson, who is perhaps best informed as to the facts, to reply to my question.'

Mr. JAMESON: 'I think ….that twelve years hence, with a building scheme attached to it, the site should be worth anything from £50,000 to £100,000.'

Leave given to withdraw Bill.

4th May, 1927. Industrial and Commercial Property (Protection) Bill 1926 Report Stage.

Dr. YEATS: 'I would like if the Minister would be able to deal with the difficulty that I put before him, about making some arrangements by which we would be able to confer copyright on American works excluded under our present arrangement, in order to obtain copyright in the interregnum. I have been away in connection with the Lane pictures and I was not able to go into the matter.'

Mr. McGILLIGAN: 'As I explained, in so far as our relations depend, anything we agree about can be adjusted under Section 176. In other words, this Order can be made applicable under certain conditions to America. The difficulty about the interregnum period does not lie with us. It lies in the legislation of the United States.. ...The Order made is the Order which will be enforced here under Section 176 in the interregnum period to which the section refers. We would have no difficulty with it, but under the existing legislation it is doubtful if the American President could make his Order have retrospective effect. As far as we can arrange things on this side this arrangement will be made.'

4th May, 1927. Industrial and Commercial Property (Protection) Bill (Resumed).

Mr. DOWDALL: 'I cannot understand the divergent views of the lawyers on this question. I believe the Berne Convention is to meet in Rome this year. As we have waited so long, it might be well to have the copyright section deleted or amended in the sense that I wish and let our representative get a decisive ruling at the Convention if we are in and Canada out, both countries having the same provisions. Some time ago I bought an Anthology of Irish verse. The compiler paid a tribute to the assistance he got from Senator Yeats. That book was published by Macmillans and was printed in England. It contained a considerable number of theses which could not be copyright owing to the lapse of time. It also contained 60 contributions in which copyright existed, and the compiler paid a tribute to the authors' indulgence in allowing him to reproduce them. The contributions of other people in which no copyright existed were reproduced in England and published there, and copyright was claimed for the whole lot. I submit that if there was such a provision as is embodied in my amendment, that abuse of copyright would not be permitted. This matter was dealt with at considerable length on the Committee Stage. We were told in the Press and by Senator Yeats at considerable length that this was an illiterate country in which no one reads. He assured us he would go to the Border if this amendment were carried. If that is true, what is the object of proposing this amendment?'

Dr. YEATS: 'I am in great difficulty. I discussed all this fully on the Committee Stage, but it seems I shall have to discuss it again and bore the House very much. I asked Senator Brown whether he thought I could omit my discussion of it and he thinks the matter of such importance that I must re-discuss the whole thing again.'

Mr. CUMMINS: 'Possibly I should not say a violent onslaught, but he subjected them to severe criticism, and, in fact, we were branded almost as an illiterate nation, not worth printing for. He drew a pathetic picture of an author to publish whose book various attempts were made in certain countries. I shall not name the author. Neither did Senator Yeats name the author, and I am glad because of the delicacy and the sensitiveness——'

Dr. YEATS: 'James Joyce.'

Mr. CUMMINS:' —— and the literary taste of the people of this country, that he did not name the author upon whose behalf a petition was signed by the highbrows——'

Dr. YEATS: 'By 150 of the most eminent men in Europe.'

Mr. CUMMINS: 'By the most eminent men in Europe, if he prefers the title. The picture was drawn to play on the feelings of members of this House to such an extent that he secured the object he was aiming at. The object that Senator Dowdall's amendment would secure is that Irish authors resident in Ireland should before they secure copyright in their own country have at least the book printed in this country. I would like to ask Senator Yeats to give us the history of the book which he spoke of in such feeling terms on the last occasion. I would ask him is it true that the British Post Office authorities have really refused to send this book through their channels, that it has been actually refused in America, that the indelicacy and the outrageous character of that book were of such a nature that it would not be permitted to go through the ordinary channels of delivery in any Christian country? There are eminent men in various countries, many eminent men in literature, eminent men in science, eminent men in Christian life, and I shall leave it to this House to judge which is the greater eminence, Christian eminence or the eminence that would destroy all semblance of Christianity on the face of the earth? The Senator tells us that this appeal is sufficiently strong to influence this House, but if this House is influenced by the appeal, it will be a surprise for the gods.'

Dr. YEATS: 'I think on the whole I shall speak. I think the Senator is quite correct. I do not like it to be supposed that I did not mention the name of James Joyce because the book was a discredit to him. I did not mention the name, because it had nothing to do with the issue. Some 150 of the most eminent men in Europe signed the protest against the mutilation and piracy of James Joyce's book in America. Some of these men sincerely admired that book and thought it a very great book. Some of those who signed the protest did not admire it at all and signed it simply because of the copyright issue. I know of one case, certainly, where a very eminent person disapproved greatly of the book, but his signature was given because of the copyright issue. American publishers had a perfect right to print that book according to the law, because it was not copyright in America. Reputable American publishers do not so pirate work. There are more or less disreputable publishers who do. There is a publisher called Roothe who pirated this book of James Joyce. I am not going to defend James Joyce. It is a very difficult question. Has the Senator ever looked into Rabelais? Rabelais is looked upon as one of the greatest masters of the past, and what is to be said of James Joyce may be said of Rabelais.

I would point out to the Senator that attached to this petition is the name of Gentile, the Italian Minister of Education, who has restored religious teaching to the schools in Italy. Another who signed this was the great Catholic philosopher of Spain, Unamuno. Does he think, leaving aside these men of special religious achievement, that there is nothing to be said for a book or a man testified to by the head of the Spanish Academy, the President of the famous Russian Academy of Letters, by various members of the French Academy of great eminence, and by the greatest living mathematician, Einstein? When I heard the Senator put up Irish opinions as against these, as certainly and definitely right, then I was inclined to believe this was an illiterate nation. These things cannot be settled as easily as that. I do not know whether Joyce's "Ulysses" is a great work of literature. I have puzzled a great deal over that question.'

CATHAOIRLEACH: 'We are travelling too far. We are not discussing this book.'

Dr. YEATS: 'All I will say is that it is the work of an heroic mind. I think Senator Dowdall acted without due thought in bringing forward this amendment. I was visited by an eminent Irish scholar who asked me to urge the House to throw out this printing clause in the interests of Irish scholarship, very largely in the interests of Irish Gaelic scholarship. Certain Irish books on phonetics are printed in Copenhagen and Germany because the characters do not exist in any Irish printing office. If this clause were passed, then in the case of those books written by Irishmen those firms would lose their Irish copyright.

He then however passed on to a very much more serious thing. Most of the work of scholarship has to be published at certain great presses which are subventioned, the Clarendon Press at Oxford and the University Press at Cambridge. We may take it that no Irish printer or publisher would deal with that kind of scholarship at all, for such works have a very small immediate sale. The sale is so small that it would not pay an Irish publisher to print those works without a subvention from the State or the University. But we are all thinking of the future. We are hoping that in the course of the next twenty or thirty years a very considerable reading public will grow up in this country. You are dealing with property which lasts not only for the lifetime of the author but for fifty years after his death. Some of the work of the scholars may be valuable property which they should have the right to leave to their children. If you pass this law you will pass a law which will injure Irish scholars. You will deprive those scholars of a copyright which may grow to be of great monetary value. We differ from Canada because in Canada there is a publishing centre and wealthy Universities. I think there are endowed University presses there. Furthermore, there is nothing in Canada like the great Irish republic of Letters which has grown up here for two centuries. One of the few means by which an Irish scholar can make money is by contributing to certain great collective publications like the universal histories now being published at the Cambridge Press. There are three great universal histories, ancient, modern and mediaeval, being published in many volumes by that Press. In those volumes portions are by separate scholars. Some are by Irish scholars. There is no possibility of getting those printed in Ireland. An Irish publisher could take out a whole section of one of those books dealing with Ireland and pirate it here. If there were no piracy then the Senator's printing clause would be inoperative. It is a clause which the whole world will regard as an incitement to piracy. There are also such compilations as the "Dictionary of National Biography," and the "Encyclopædia Britannica." Several of our Irish scholars have worked on these for many years.

There are always new editions. Universal histories will always be produced. The whole publishing and printing system by which Irish scholars live will be upset not only in dealing with these great compilations but in connection with another side of the question which Senator Dowdall has not thought of. If his final amendment down on the Paper is carried no Irish writer will be able to serialise his work in England. A young novelist will not be able to publish his stories in the "Windsor" or "Pall Mall" magazines. I have mentioned a case in which an eminent Irish writer has just finished an important autobiography which in the ordinary course of events would be published in an English newspaper. That work could be pirated here. The Irish newspapers might take out large sections. What would happen to an Irish author? He sends a story to the "Windsor Magazine." The "Windsor Magazine" says: "No, we cannot publish it; you are a citizen of the Free State." Someone in Ireland would pirate the story and then the right Senator Dowdall proposes to confer upon that person could exclude the "Windsor Magazine" from Ireland. Not only are you giving the Irish publisher the right to pirate sections from the magazines, newspapers, the great universal histories, the "Dictionary of National Biography," and "Encyclopædia Britannica," but you are going to give him the right to exclude from Ireland these publications. The thing is laughable. A sane man should not give two minutes' thought to the amendment. What are you going to gain in the end? If you have all the Irish writers that exist printing here in Dublin they are not sufficient to keep your printing presses busy for half a year.'

Mr. DOWDALL: What is your authority for saying that?

Dr. YEATS: 'I cannot give statistics. I know pretty well who the Irish authors are whose works have some value in the market. They are not very numerous. If you get them all you cannot make a successful centre of printing in Ireland unless you get English publishers to print here. At this moment one of the Irish printers is successfully printing a number of popular novels for an English publisher. What will happen when you commit the first conspicuous act of piracy? There is a body called the Publishers' Association and another the Society of Authors. What will happen will be on a very much larger scale than what happened in the case of that pirated book in America when 150 authors protested not only to American sentiment but also made an appeal to American publishers to withdraw advertisements from a particular journal. What will happen will be far greater because action will come through the English Publishers' Association and the Society of Authors. Your entire printing will be snuffed out and you will outrage the opinion of the world as Canada has not, because you will be the first European nation to break in upon the accord of Europe on the subject of intellectual property.

America is moving towards the European position. As late as thirty years ago there was practically no copyright in America. The works of the most eminent writers, such as Dickens and Thackeray, were pirated. It was a world scandal. Then gradually the finer tastes of America were able to assert themselves and the Copyright Act was passed. No educated American looks upon that as final, but that it is simply moving towards the European position. Naturally, perhaps, Canada adopted the same law, which deals not only with Canadian but with American citizens. You will be very different. You will not be moving from a condition of piracy, but towards it, and you will bring upon your head an amount of obloquy of which you have no idea. I do not want to close with what the Senator calls "negation." Ireland is now, intellectually, in the position Edinburgh was at the beginning of the nineteenth century. Gradually Edinburgh became a great centre of publishing and printing. Edinburgh had great intellectual prestige. We have given you intellectual prestige. It will be your fault if you do not make Dublin a great centre of printing, but you will not make it a great centre of printing unless you retain the good-will of the publishers and writers of England and the British Empire.'

Amendment put and negatived.

18th July, 1928. Constitution (Amendment No.6) Bill, 1928, Fifth Stage.

Dr. YEATS: 'I think we should not lose sight of the simple fact that it is more desirable and more important to have able men in this House than to get representative men into this House. Looking down the list of Senators who will be going up for re-election—I am not one of them—I am certain that the ablest men on that list stand a better opportunity of returning to this House if this Bill be passed, than they would stand if the Bill be not passed.'

The PRESIDENT: 'This Bill embodies one of the recommendations of the Joint Committee which sat to consider——'

Conclusion

W.B. Yeats was world renowned for his contribution to literature. Yeats was awarded the Nobel Prize for Literature in 1923. Yeats, maintained nostalgia for the tradition of his own Anglo-Irish Protestant gentry and nobility which were his origins and his speeches reflect that origin thus remaining unknown, so, this book makes them available for a wider, younger and discerning audience. Yeats was the master orator readily and easily converting his opponents consistently to his side.

Yeats supported James Joyce's right to US copyright when his book, Ulysses, was published and faced much controversy in 1922. Yeats ensured the Hugh Lane paintings were shared between Ireland and England in the absence of a will or bequest when Lane died on the USS Lusitania in 1915. Yeats pioneered the adoption of the animal themed coinage which remains fondly in the memories of Irish people through the generations. Yeats sharp wit fully tested the endurance of his fellow Senators when he decried Parnell's dalliance with a married woman and Lord Nelson, who tarried with Lady Hamilton, he propose to be hanged for adultery. O'Connell, who remained married, gained much invective from Yeats, who claimed one could hit a scion of O'Connell by casting said stick over the workhouse wall.

Overall Yeats gave us some of the most quoted poetry in the language:

'..but I being poor, have only my dreams; I have spread my dreams under your feet; Tread softly because you tread on my dreams.'

'No country for old men; A terrible beauty is born; To the waters and the wild; The light of evening Lisaddel; Great hatred, little room.

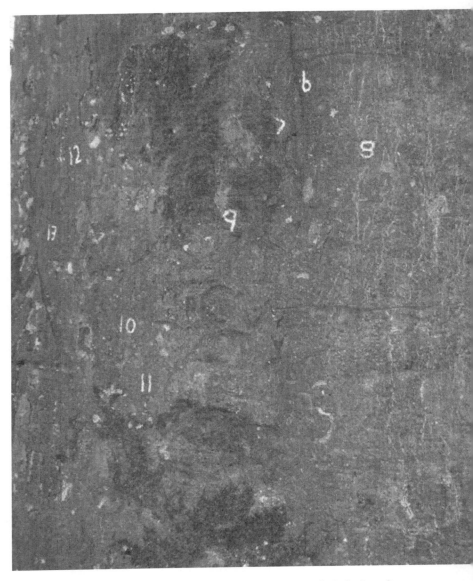

W.B.Yeats autograph (10) on the Copper Beech autograph tree Coole Park, Gort, Co Galway. W right of 10, B green moss and Y obvious to right.

Thoor Ballylee near Gort, Co Galway, the Norman Tower purchased by Yeats in 1919 and where he lived each summer until 1932 and where he prepared his Seanad Eireann speeches 1922 until 1928.

Seanad Members Database 1922-25

Mr. John Philip Bagwell
Nominated by the President of the Executive Council
Party: Independent *(Independent members of the 1922 Seanad)*

- **Dr. Henry Leo Barniville**
  Elected
  Party: Independent *(Independent members of the 1922 Seanad)*
- **Mr. William Barrington**
  Elected
  Party: Independent *(Independent members of the 1922 Seanad)*
- **Mr. Thomas Westropp Bennett**
  Elected
  Party: Independent *(Independent members of the 1922 Seanad)*
- **Mr. Samuel Lombard Brown, K.C.**
  Elected
  Party: Independent *(Independent members of the 1922 Seanad)*
- **Rt. Hon. Henry Givens Burgess**
  Elected
  Party: Independent *(Independent members of the 1922 Seanad)*
- **Mr. Richard. A Butler**
  Elected
  Party: Independent *(Independent members of the 1922 Seanad)*
- **Mrs. Eileen (Ellen) Costello**
  Elected
  Party: Independent *(Independent members of the 1922 Seanad)*
- **Mr. John Joseph Counihan**
  Elected
  Party: Independent *(Independent members of the 1922 Seanad)*
- **Mr. William Cummins**
  Elected
  Party: Independent *(Independent members of the 1922 Seanad)*
- **Mr. Peter De Loughry**
  Elected
  Party: Independent *(Independent members of the 1922 Seanad)*
- **Countess of Desart**
  Nominated by the President of the Executive Council
  Party: Independent *(Independent members of the 1922 Seanad)*

- **Mr. James Green Douglas**
  Elected
  Party: Independent *(Independent members of the 1922 Seanad)*
- **Mr. James Charles Dowdall**
  Nominated by the President of the Executive Council
  Party: Independent *(Independent members of the 1922 Seanad)*
- **Mr. Michael Duffy**
  Elected
  Party: The Labour Party *(The Labour Party members of the 1922 Seanad)*
- **Earl of Dunraven**
  Nominated by the President of the Executive Council
  Party: Independent *(Independent members of the 1922 Seanad)*
- **Sir Thomas Henry Grattan Esmonde, Bart.**
  Nominated by the President of the Executive Council
  Party: Independent *(Independent members of the 1922 Seanad)*
- **Sir Nugent Talbot Everard, Bart.**
  Nominated by the President of the Executive Council
  Party: Independent *(Independent members of the 1922 Seanad)*
- **Mr. Edmund W. Eyre**
  Nominated by the President of the Executive Council
  Party: Independent *(Independent members of the 1922 Seanad)*
- **Mr. Thomas Farren**
  Elected
  Party: The Labour Party *(The Labour Party members of the 1922 Seanad)*
- **Mr. Martin Fitzgerald**
  Elected
- **Mr. Thomas Foran**
  Elected
  Party: Independent *(Independent members of the 1922 Seanad)*
- **Lord Glenavy**
  Nominated by the President of the Executive Council
  Party: Cathaoirleach *(Website / Cathaoirleach members of the 1922 Seanad)*
- **Dr. Oliver St. John Gogarty**
  Nominated by the President of the Executive Council
- **Mr. James Perry Goodbody**
  Nominated by the President of the Executive Council
- **Earl of Granard**
  Nominated by the President of the Executive Council

- **Mrs. Alice Stopford Green**
  - Elected
  - **Party:** Independent *(Independent members of the 1922 Seanad)*
- **Capt. Henry Greer ***
  - Elected
  - **Party:** Independent *(Independent members of the 1922 Seanad)*
- **Sir John Purser Griffith**
  - Elected
  - **Party:** Independent *(Independent members of the 1922 Seanad)*
- **Mr. Henry Seymour Guinness**
  - Elected
  - **Party:** Independent *(Independent members of the 1922 Seanad)*
- **Mr. Benjamin Haughton**
  - Elected
  - **Party:** Independent *(Independent members of the 1922 Seanad)*
- **Dr. Douglas Hyde**
  - Elected
  - **Party:** Independent *(Independent members of the 1922 Seanad)*
- **Mr. Cornelius J. Irwin**
  - Elected
  - **Party:** Independent *(Independent members of the 1922 Seanad)*
- **Mr. Arthur Jackson**
  - Nominated by the President of the Executive Council
- **Rt. Hon. Andrew Jameson**
  - Nominated by the President of the Executive Council
- **Sir John Keane, Bart.**
  - Nominated by the President of the Executive Council
- **Mr. Patrick W. Kenny**
  - Elected
  - **Party:** Independent *(Independent members of the 1922 Seanad)*
- **Earl of Kerry ***
  - Nominated by the President of the Executive Council
- **Mr. Thomas Linehan**
  - Elected
  - **Party:** Independent *(Independent members of the 1922 Seanad)*
- **Mr. Joseph Clayton Love**
  - Elected
  - **Party:** Independent *(Independent members of the 1922 Seanad)*
- **Mr. Edward MacEvoy**
  - Elected
  - **Party:** Independent *(Independent members of the 1922 Seanad)*

- **Mr. James J. MacKean**
  Elected
  Party: Independent *(Independent members of the 1922 Seanad)*
- **Mr. John MacLoughlin**
  Elected
  Party: Independent *(Independent members of the 1922 Seanad)*
- **Mr. Edward MacLysaght**
  Elected
  Party: Independent *(Independent members of the 1922 Seanad)*
- **Mr. Thomas MacPartlin**
  Elected
  Party: The Labour Party *(The Labour Party members of the 1922 Seanad)*
- **Rt. Hon. Sir Bryan Mahon**
  Nominated by the President of the Executive Council
- **Mr. Edward Mansfield**
  Elected
  Party: The Labour Party *(The Labour Party members of the 1922 Seanad)*
- **Marquess of Headfort**
  Nominated by the President of the Executive Council
- **Earl of Mayo**
  Nominated by the President of the Executive Council
- **Mr. William John Molloy**
  Elected
  Party: Independent *(Independent members of the 1922 Seanad)*
- **Colonel Maurice George Moore**
  Elected
  Party: Independent *(Independent members of the 1922 Seanad)*
- **Mr. James Moran**
  Nominated by the President of the Executive Council
- **Mr. George Nesbitt**
  Elected
  Party: Independent *(Independent members of the 1922 Seanad)*
- **Mr. Michael O'Dea**
  Elected
  Party: Independent *(Independent members of the 1922 Seanad)*
- **Mr. John Thomas O'Farrell**
  Elected
  Party: The Labour Party *(The Labour Party members of the 1922 Seanad)*

- **Mr. John O'Neill**
  Elected
  Party: Independent *(Independent members of the 1922 Seanad)*
- **Mr. Brian O'Rourke**
  Elected
  Party: Independent *(Independent members of the 1922 Seanad)*
- **Dr. William O'Sullivan**
  Elected
  Party: Independent *(Independent members of the 1922 Seanad)*
- **Mr. James Joseph Parkinson**
  Elected
  Party: Independent *(Independent members of the 1922 Seanad)*
- **Sir Horace Plunkett**
  Nominated by the President of the Executive Council
- **Sir William Hutcheson Poë**
  Nominated by the President of the Executive Council
- **Mrs. Jane Wyse Power**
  Nominated by the President of the Executive Council
- **Dr. George Sigerson**
  Nominated by the President of the Executive Council
- **Earl of Wicklow**
  Nominated by the President of the Executive Council
- **Mr. William Butler Yeats**
  Nominated by the President of the Executive Council
  Party: Independent *(Independent members of the 1922 Seanad)*

Seanad Members Database 1925-28

Mr. John Philip Bagwell
Nominated by the President of the Executive Council
Party: Independent *(Independent members of the 1925Seanad)*

- **Dr. Henry Leo Barniville**
  Elected
  Party: Independent *(Independent members of the 1925 Seanad)*
- **Mr. William Barrington**
  Elected
  Party: Independent *(Independent members of the 1925 Seanad)*
- **Sir Edward Bellingham, Bart.**
  Elected
- **Mr. Thomas Westropp Bennett**
  Elected
  Party: Independent *(Independent members of the 1925 Seanad)*
- **Sir Edward Coey Bigger**
  Elected
- **Mr. Patrick. J Brady**
  Elected
- **Mr. Samuel Lombard Brown, K.C.**
  Elected
  Party: Independent *(Independent members of the 1925 Seanad)*
- **Rt. Hon. Henry Givens Burgess**
  Elected
  Party: Independent *(Independent members of the 1925 Seanad)*
- **Mrs. Eileen (Ellen) Costello**
  Elected
  Party: Independent *(Independent members of the 1925 Seanad)*
- **Mr. John Joseph Counihan**
  Elected
  Party: Independent *(Independent members of the 1925 Seanad)*
- **Mr. William Cummins**
  Elected
  Party: Independent *(Independent members of the 1925 Seanad)*
- **Countess of Desart**
  Nominated by the President of the Executive Council
  Party: Independent *(Independent members of the 1925 Seanad)*
- **Mr. James Dillon**
  Elected

- **Mr. James Green Douglas**
  Elected
  Party: Independent *(Independent members of the 1925 Seanad)*
- **Mr. James Charles Dowdall**
  Nominated by the President of the Executive Council
  Party: Independent *(Independent members of the 1925 Seanad)*
- **Mr. Michael Duffy**
  Elected
  Party: The Labour Party *(The Labour Party members of the 1925 Seanad)*
- **Earl of Dunraven**
  Nominated by the President of the Executive Council
  Party: Independent *(Independent members of the 1925 Seanad)*
- **Sir Thomas Henry Grattan Esmonde, Bart.**
  Nominated by the President of the Executive Council
  Party: Independent *(Independent members of the 1925 Seanad)*
- **Sir Nugent Talbot Everard, Bart.**
  Nominated by the President of the Executive Council
  Party: Independent *(Independent members of the 1925 Seanad)*
- **Mr. Edmund W. Eyre**
  Nominated by the President of the Executive Council
  Party: Independent *(Independent members of the 1925 Seanad)*
- **Mr. Michael Fanning**
  Elected
- **Mr. Thomas Farren**
  Elected
  Party: The Labour Party *(The Labour Party members of the 1925 Seanad)*
- **Mr. Martin Fitzgerald**
  Elected
- **Mr. Thomas Foran**
  Elected
  Party: Independent *(Independent members of the 1925 Seanad)*
- **Lord Glenavy**
  Nominated by the President of the Executive Council
  Party: Cathaoirleach *(Website / Cathaoirleach members of the 1925 Seanad)*
- **Dr. Oliver St. John Gogarty**
  Nominated by the President of the Executive Council
- **Mr. James Perry Goodbody**
  Nominated by the President of the Executive Council
- **Earl of Granard**
  Nominated by the President of the Executive Council

- **Mrs. Alice Stopford Green**
  Elected
  Party: Independent *(Independent members of the 1925 Seanad)*
- **Capt. Henry Greer ***
  Elected
  Party: Independent *(Independent members of the 1925 Seanad)*
- **Sir John Purser Griffith**
  Elected
  Party: Independent *(Independent members of the 1925 Seanad)*
- **Mr. Henry Seymour Guinness**
  Elected
  Party: Independent *(Independent members of the 1925 Seanad)*
- **Mr. Benjamin Haughton**
  Elected
  Party: Independent *(Independent members of the 1925 Seanad)*
- **Sir William Hickie**
  Elected
- **Mr. Patrick Joseph Hooper**
  Elected
- **Mr. Arthur Jackson**
  Nominated by the President of the Executive Council
- **Rt. Hon. Andrew Jameson**
  Nominated by the President of the Executive Council
- **Sir John Keane, Bart.**
  Nominated by the President of the Executive Council
- **Mr. Cornelius Kennedy**
  Elected
- **Mr. Patrick W. Kenny**
  Elected
  Party: Independent *(Independent members of the 1925 Seanad)*
- **Earl of Kerry ***
  Nominated by the President of the Executive Council
- **Mr. Thomas Linehan**
  Elected
  Party: Independent *(Independent members of the 1925 Seanad)*
- **Mr. Francis MacGuinness**
  Elected
  Party: Sinn Féin (Pro-Treaty) *(Sinn Féin (Pro-Treaty) members of the 1925 Seanad)*
- **Mr. James J. MacKean**
  Elected
  Party: Independent *(Independent members of the 1925 Seanad)*

- **Mr. John MacLoughlin**
  Elected
  Party: Independent *(Independent members of the 1925 Seanad)*
- **Rt. Hon. Sir Bryan Mahon**
  Nominated by the President of the Executive Council
- **Marquess of Headfort**
  Nominated by the President of the Executive Council
- **Earl of Mayo**
  Nominated by the President of the Executive Council
- **Mr. William John Molloy**
  Elected
  Party: Independent *(Independent members of the 1925 Seanad)*
- **Colonel Maurice George Moore**
  Elected
  Party: Independent *(Independent members of the 1925 Seanad)*
- **Mr. James Moran**
  Nominated by the President of the Executive Council
- **Sir Walter Nugent, Bart.**
  Elected
- **Mr. Joseph O'Connor**
  Elected
- **Mr. John Thomas O'Farrell**
  Elected
  Party: The Labour Party *(The Labour Party members of the 1925 Seanad)*
- **Mr. Michael F. O'Hanlon,**
  Elected
- **Mr. Stephen O'Mara**
  Elected
- **Mr. Brian O'Rourke**
  Elected
  Party: Independent *(Independent members of the 1925 Seanad)*
- **Dr. William O'Sullivan**
  Elected
  Party: Independent *(Independent members of the 1925 Seanad)*
- **Mr. James Joseph Parkinson**
  Elected
  Party: Independent *(Independent members of the 1925 Seanad)*
- **Mrs. Jane Wyse Power**
  Nominated by the President of the Executive Council
- **Mr. Thomas Toal**
  Elected

- **Earl of Wicklow**
  Nominated by the President of the Executive Council
- **Mr. William Butler Yeats**
  Nominated by the President of the Executive Council
  Party: Independent *(Independent members of the 1925 Seanad)*

References:

W.B. Yeats, Irish Independent Great Biographies, Augustine Martin

The Collected Poems of W. B. Yeats, Wordsworth Poetry Library

Soundings, Augustine Martin, Gill and MacMillan

The Cosgrave Party, a History of Cumann na nGaedhael, 1923 – 33, Ciara Meehan

The Life of W.B. Yeats, Terence Brown, Gill and Macmillan

W.B. Yeats Man and Poet, A. .Norman Jeffares, Kyle Cathie Limited

Seanad Eireann Membership Sources

http://www.oireachtas.ie/members-hist/default.asp?housetype=1&HouseNum=1922&disp=mem

http://www.oireachtas.ie/members-hist/default.asp?housetype=1&HouseNum=1925&disp=mem

Seanad Eireann debates and speeches

- Volume 1 (11/12/1922 - 09/08/1923)
- Volume 2 (19/09/1923 - 03/04/1924)
- Volume 3 (01/05/1924 - 19/12/1924)
- Volume 4 (21/01/1925 - 07/04/1925)
- Volume 5 (30/04/1925 - 08/07/1925)
- Volume 6 (09/12/1925 - 31/03/1926)
- Volume 7 (28/04/1926 - 24/11/1926)
- Volume 8 (15/12/1926 - 20/05/1927)
- Volume 9 (23/06/1927 - 10/08/1927)
- Volume 10 (11/10/1927 - 28/11/1928)